LISTENING TO THE LEAST

LISTENING TO THE LEAST

doing theology from the outside in

Ian A. McFarland

UNITED CHURCH PRESS Cleveland, Ohio

The Pilgrim Press, Cleveland, Ohio 44115
© 1998 by Ian A. McFarland

From James H. Cone, *God of the Oppressed*. Revised edition published by Orbis Books.
Copyright 1997 by James H. Cone. Reprinted by permission. • From Hans W. Frei,
The Identity of Jesus Christ: The Hermeneutical Bases of Dogmatic Theology (Fortress Press,
1975). Reprinted by permission of Geraldine Frei. • From Ian A. McFarland, "The
Ecstatic God: The Holy Spirit and the Constitution of the Trinity," *Theology Today* 54
(October 1997): 335–46. Reprinted by permission from *Theology Today*.

03   02   01   00   99   98   5   4   3   2   1

Library of Congress Cataloging-in-Publication Data
McFarland, Ian A. (Ian Alexander), 1963–
    Listening to the least : doing theology from the outside in / Ian
A. McFarland.
        p.   cm.
    Includes bibliographical references and index.
    ISBN 0-8298-1283-0 (paper : alk. paper)
    1. Church—Authority.   2. Protestant churches—Doctrines.   3. Afro-
American churches.   I. Title.
BT91.M34   1998
262'.8—dc21   98-36234
                                                    CIP

LET THE BELIEVER WHO IS LOWLY BOAST IN

BEING RAISED UP, AND THE RICH IN BEING BROUGHT LOW.

—James 1:9–10 (NRSV)

CONTENTS

ACKNOWLEDGMENTS

This book has been a long time in the making and, in the process, has undergone a number of revisions, some more extensive than others. It had its beginnings almost ten years ago in the course of my preparing a sermon while serving as parish intern at Grace Lutheran Church in Muscatine, Iowa. I went on to deepen and develop these early ideas as a graduate student at Yale University. But it was once again in the parish context—this time in preparing an adult education series at the Lutheran Church of Honolulu—that the argument came together in more or less final form.

Given the emphasis I place in the book on the significance of community in biblical interpretation, I find it theologically as well as personally significant that two of the book's major themes (the metaphor of God working from the outside in and my interpretation of trinitarian doctrine) emerged so directly from my own sharing in the life of these congregations. I am happy to have this occasion to thank the members of both communities for the many ways in which they have deepened my faith and enriched my life beyond the preparation of this manuscript.

I owe an immense debt to my teachers and colleagues at Yale and elsewhere for the faithful and, I fear, often underappreciated ways in which they have given this book whatever merit it may have. First among equals in this list is Kathryn Tanner, who patiently waded through countless drafts of the manuscript, providing invaluable criticism and even greater support at every turn. My deepest thanks also go to Renée Hill, Serene Jones, David Kelsey, George Lindbeck, and Christopher Morse, whose insights helped me over many rough patches in working out both form and content. The reader should be assured that the responsibility for whatever shortcomings remain (and I am afraid there are all too many) rests entirely with me.

I would also like to express my gratitude to Timothy Staveteig, Ed Huddleston, and the many other people at Pilgrim Press whose names remain unknown to me, but without whose contributions this book could not have been produced. Special thanks are due also to the editors of *Theology Today* for permission to use material on the doctrine of the Trinity from an article originally published in the October 1997 issue of their journal.

My final and deepest appreciation remains for my wife, Ann, who consciously chose to have as little as possible to do with this project and thereby reminded me that there are more important and more lasting things in life than the making of books.

INTRODUCTION

This book is a defense of the authority of Jesus Christ and of his disciples. In this sense, its aims are apologetic. Yet it takes as given the truth of Christian belief about Jesus. It is therefore not apologetic in the sense in which that word has generally been used over the last two hundred years.

This does not mean that I take Christian faith in Jesus to be self-evident. That Jesus is the Christ, and therefore the one to whom "all authority on heaven and earth" has been given, is arguably Christianity's defining belief. But Jesus' authority is, after all, the authority of a dead man; and his followers' claim that this man was raised from the dead does little to commend their position in the eyes of most outside observers. Moreover, even if Jesus' authority is accepted, it remains far from clear that those who call themselves Christians have the right to preach and teach in Jesus' name.

All the same, the explanation of Christian faith presented in this book will not take the form of an attempt to prove the truth of the Christian faith in light of premises supposed to be binding upon all rational persons. Nor will I try to show that Christianity is meaningful, in the sense that it can be shown to address certain basic questions about existence in some significant way. Admittedly, I would probably not have much interest in defending Jesus' authority—not to mention that of the church—if I personally did not find Christianity both meaningful and true. But insofar as faith in Jesus

Christ is understood to be a gift of the Holy Spirit, its truth would seem by its very nature incapable of objective proof. The aim of this piece of apologetics is therefore not to prove the truth of the faith to non-Christians. Instead, my aim is to clarify the nature of Christian claims and thereby, perhaps, remove certain misunderstandings regarding the nature and scope of those claims that have taken root inside and outside the churches. The strategy I have adopted is dictated less by general criteria of rationality than by the particular situation in which the church is asked to preach. As a true *apologia,* or courtroom defense, this book is intended to answer a specific set of challenges facing those who would preach the gospel in contemporary North America and not to provide a universal defense of the faith designed to meet all comers.[1]

The challenges with which I am concerned center on the question of the authority Christians claim for their words and actions. It is a natural part of any human enterprise that people seek to give reasons for acting in one way rather than another, and Christianity is no different. To the extent that theology can be understood as a tool Christians use in order to give an account of their behavior, examining the Christian concept of authority includes reflection on what counts as good theological reasoning. Once again, this is not a matter of trying show Christianity's superiority to other systems of belief, but of making a case for how authority should be understood in a specifically Christian context. In other words, by arguing for a particular way of understanding authority within the church, I am proposing a particular way of *being* a Christian, not giving reasons for *becoming* one. That Jesus is the Christ is, as already noted, a matter of faith that I doubt is capable of proof. But the question of *what it means to claim* that Jesus is the Christ is unavoidable for Christians as they make concrete decisions about their life as a community of faith.

The church's authority is widely questioned. Outside of the churches, rationalists of various stripes have dismissed the claims of Christianity as a more or less dangerous collection of superstitions. Within the churches, there has been considerable confusion as to where authority lies and what form it should take. And for people everywhere, the legacy of the church's implicit and explicit endorsements of serfdom, slavery, colonialism, anti-Semitism, and any number of oppressive political regimes stands as a powerful objection to Christian claims to be able to speak with authority. All these considerations call for some clarification of the sort of authority Christians claim.

This question is addressed in a series of seven chapter-length essays that, taken together, amount to a way of understanding authority in Christian faith. While the range of topics explored varies considerably from chapter to chapter, each chapter centers on some aspect of the relationship between the human and the divine exercise of authority. This question is important because Christians have, in general, wanted to claim divine authority as the basis for their preaching of the gospel without presuming to equate their authority with God's. Satisfying both these conditions means walking a very fine line when it comes to claiming authority: if Christians claim too little, they undermine their rationale for teaching at all; but if they claim too much, they belie the content of their preaching by failing to distinguish God as the source of their message from themselves as messengers.

Chapter 1 begins the process by exploring the logic of authority in Christian belief by examining the doctrine of revelation, which has been the means by which most theologians in the modern era have attempted to defend Christian claims to teach with authority. More often than not, the topic of revelation has been treated using the tools of philosophy to show that Christian claims to revealed knowledge are defensible in terms of general principles of rationality. Although none of these efforts have proven widely persuasive, the very fact of this consistent failure makes the doctrine of revelation a natural starting point for systematic reflection on Christian claims to teach with authority. The results of this analysis suggest that the proponents of a doctrine of revelation have attempted both too much and too little. They have attempted too much to the extent that they have often mistaken the task of theology as that of providing a global defense of Christianity in terms of allegedly universal truths of reason. They have attempted too little in that they have neglected to let theology's own sources challenge models of knowledge and authority imported from non-Christian systems of thought.

In light of this failure of philosophically based appeals to revelation, chapter 2 attempts to sketch out some of the defining issues for a specifically Christian understanding of authority. Chief among these is the fact that theology points away from the church to the work of God in Christ and, at the same time, necessarily refers to the church as the context within which God in Christ continues to claim human beings. The tension between these Christocentric and ecclesiocentric dimensions of theological language are explored with special reference to the legacy of African American Christianity, which is notable for seeming to combine both a strong emphasis on the priority of Christ with an equally powerful sense of the role of the community as the matrix within which Christ's sovereignty assumes definite form and in terms of which claims to speak in Christ's name may be judged.

In chapter 3, the apparent opposition between the Christocentric and ecclesiocentric dimensions of theology is explored in greater depth through an extended analysis of the Reformation principle of Scripture alone, or *sola Scriptura*. In response to what they viewed as an excess of ecclesiocentrism on the part of the Catholic establishment, the Reformers insisted upon the hermeneutical priority and sufficiency of Scripture as the definitive witness to Jesus Christ. Yet, as the Reformers themselves acknowledged, to insist on the priority of Scripture is not necessarily to deny that the church functions as a necessary context for the faithful reading of Scripture. In this context, the Reformers' insistence on scriptural priority requires further clarification in light of the difficulty of separating a community's openness to God's Word in Scripture from its commitment to particular traditions of interpretation within which Scripture is read as the Word of God.

In this discussion, too, the black churches provide an important theological reference point. While African American Christians have from the time of slavery treated the Bible as the supreme authority in matters of faith, the fact that they do so is intimately linked to their experience of Scripture's ability to give dignity to a community subject to systematic degradation by the larger, white-dominated society. No contradiction was experienced in this combination of practices, because black Christians understood the

Bible's story (and, in particular, Jesus' story) as their own. Nor did this conviction result from allowing the community's experience to eclipse the biblical witness. Quite the contrary, it was motivated precisely by the recognition that Scripture itself portrayed Jesus as one whose identity is inseparable from the ongoing story of the covenant community. That is, the community did not claim authority *over against* Jesus, but *on the basis of the fact that* Jesus' own authority is depicted and encountered in Scripture as inseparable from the life of the community.

African American Christians' sense of the communal matrix of Scripture suggests a basic continuity between divine authority manifest in Jesus Christ and the human authority of the church. By itself, this conclusion might appear to imply a fatal confusion of God and the church. Chapter 4 discusses the Reformers' attempts to avoid such confusion by proposing various "marks" that distinguish the true church from false claimants. While I believe that their proposed solutions to this problem fall short, they do suggest that the identity (and thus the authority) of the church is determined not only by *what* its members believe (orthodoxy) but also by *how* they believe it (orthopraxy).

Having reviewed in the first half of the book some of the more important questions associated with Christian claims to teach with authority, chapter 5 constructs a model of theological authority in light of the conclusions reached in earlier chapters. I take as my point of departure the observation (already defended in chapter 3) that in Jesus God identifies with the community of faith. But I go on to argue that the fact of Jesus' identification with the church cannot be separated from the way in which it is accomplished. Jesus does not identify with the community through its leaders (who, on the contrary, are the objects of many of his harshest attacks), but rather through the prostitutes, tax collectors, and other sinners who live on the community's margins. It follows that Jesus' presence as Savior is not with leaders, nor even with the community in general, but precisely with those "little ones" in relation to whom his own preaching of the realm of God finds its most willing reception and thereby its decisive confirmation. In other words, while Jesus does identify with (and thereby guarantee the authority of) the community, he does so "from the outside in," building and sustaining the community from its margins rather than from the established centers of power and authority represented in the Gospels by the scribes and Pharisees.

This reversal of conventional expectations regarding the movement of authority in the community makes it possible to understand how it is possible to attribute genuine theological authority to the church without thereby placing established communal practice beyond the reach of theological criticism. Because Christ identifies with the community from the outside in, the (established) authority of the community is preserved only to the extent that it continually places itself in jeopardy, breaking down established channels of power and influence by moving to those at the community's margins. In this way, Jesus' exercise of authority justifies the conclusion that in the church, genuine authority is also exercised from the outside in.

The one remaining question is the extent to which Jesus' way of exercising authority is rooted in the being of God. For even if it is recognized that the biblical Jesus exercises authority from the outside in, the implications of this practice for the church remain theologically indeterminate unless we encounter God's own life in Jesus' ministry. Chapter 6 attempts to make this case by interpreting the doctrine of the Trinity as a summary description of the New Testament witness that the God revealed in Jesus Christ constitutes the divine being itself from the outside in. From this perspective, the resurrection is not only the vindication of Jesus (as God's "Son"), but of the God whom he calls Father, whose own identity *as* Father is at stake in Jesus' ministry at the margins.

Furthermore, because Jesus' authority is inseparable from the life of the community, the claim that God's own identity is at stake in Jesus' ministry means that the church's authority quite properly can be identified with God's own—provided that the church lives from its own margins. This argument is brought to a conclusion in chapter 7 by drawing out some of the implications of a God who lives from the margins for Christian faith and practice.

In summary, I try to show that the human exercise of authority in the church can legitimately be conceived in strict continuity with God's own exercise of authority. At the same time, I insist that close examination of the way God exercises authority (and, more profoundly, of the dynamics of the divine life itself) means that this conclusion, far from supporting any form of Christian triumphalism, undermines any claim to theological authority that is not made from a position of solidarity with those at the margins of the faith community.

Beginning with a review of the challenges that confront Christian claims to speak with authority (chapter 1), I define the central problem of the study as that of mediating between what I call Christocentric and ecclesiocentric dimensions of Christian theology (chapter 2). I then go on to explore possible ways of relating the two by analyzing the role of Scripture (chapter 3) and the identity of the church (chapter 4). Building on these analyses, I propose a model of authority rooted in the person of Christ (chapter 5) and, ultimately, in the being of God (chapter 6).

The result is an apology for Christian claims to teach with authority. This apology does not prove such claims to be justified as such, but it does defend them against the charge of being inherently dismissive of critique. On the contrary, a thorough examination of the logic of Christian belief in the sovereignty of Jesus Christ suggests that the church speaks with authority only to the extent that it allows that authority to be called into question by those who have the least share in it.

chapter one

THE PROBLEM OF AUTHORITY

"And when Jesus had finished these words, the crowds were astonished at his teaching; for he taught them as one having authority, and not as their scribes" (Matt. 7:28–29).[1] These words from the end of the Sermon on the Mount, along with parallel passages in the Gospels (for example, Mark 1:22, 27), suggest that from the beginning of his ministry, Jesus confronted those around him with the question of authority. Specifically, he forgave sin. This seems truly to have set his contemporaries on edge, because to forgive sin was implicitly to claim ultimate authority: "Who is able to forgive sins but the one God?" (Mark 2:7 and parallels). If sin is that which separates the individual from God, then to forgive sin is to overcome that separation. Small wonder, then, that the scribes ascribed such authority to God alone. Yet Jesus maintains that this authority has been granted him, and his disciples have persisted in declaring the forgiveness of sins in his name. In continuing this proclamation down through the generations, Christians claim they have a definitive word to speak to human beings of every time and place. The authority of this claim was once largely unquestioned in the Western world, but it is so no longer. On what basis do Christians make it now?

CHALLENGES TO CHRISTIAN CLAIMS OF AUTHORITY

The question of authority cannot be avoided. Where consensus regarding God, humankind, and the world is lacking, Christians have long recognized an obligation to explain why the claims of their particular tradition should be regarded as authoritative: "Sanctify . . . Christ in your hearts, being ready always to make a defense to anyone asking you for an account of the hope that is in you" (1 Pet. 3:15). Before it is possible to assess Christian claims to teach with authority, however, it is necessary to come to some preliminary understanding of what authority is. On one hand, the Gospels view authority (*exousia*) as a power that has been given to Jesus (definitively in Matt. 28:18) and which Jesus can, in turn, delegate to others (for example, in Matt. 10:1 and pars.; Luke 10:19). In certain settings, the recognition of Jesus' authority is simply a reaction to his power over the physical world (see Matt. 8:23–27 and pars.; Mark 1:22, 27; Luke 5:4–11), yet the question of Jesus' authority cannot be resolved simply by reference to these episodes, if for no other reason than that Jesus' deeds of power are open to various interpretations.[2] Indeed, it is an undeniable feature of the Gospel accounts that Jesus' authority is subject to challenge. The fact that Jesus can be asked by what authority he does what he does (Matt. 21:23 and pars.) suggests that his claim to authority includes an acknowledgment of accountability.[3] This feature of Jesus' own exercise of authority, which culminates in his submission to the brutal realities of his trial and execution,[4] directs those who would follow him to the question of that to which they hold themselves accountable.

The accountability of Christians for the authority they claim is a particularly pressing issue at the present time, when a situation of cultural pluralism means that the church (at least in its "mainline" Protestant form) can no longer take its authority in society for granted. The challenge of pluralism takes two basic forms, both of which have become major foci of theology in the last quarter of the twentieth century. First, contemporary culture confronts the church with competing claims to authority, both in the form of other religious traditions and in the claims of the social and natural sciences.[5] The question of how the church relates to these counterclaims has been a major concern of academic theology in North America and Europe, where the experience of competing claims has led to a reexamination of both the kind and the extent of the authority the church claims for its talk about Jesus of Nazareth.[6]

In its second form, the challenge to church authority emerged initially from the absence rather than the presence of competing claims. The recognition that large segments of the world's population (especially people of color and women) have been more or less systematically prevented from claiming authority for their own speech because of the power exercised by a few (usually white men) has led to a widespread reassessment of the church's authority. This reassessment has taken concrete form in the various theologies of liberation that have emerged within traditionally marginalized groups. These theologies argue that certain of the ideas and practices for which the church has claimed authority have functioned both implicitly and explicitly to exclude competing claims to authority and thus to create a false impression of consensus. To counteract this tendency, liberation theologians have proposed the reconceptualization of theology as "critical reflection on Christian praxis" that is directly concerned with the church's relations to established authority.[7]

Though these two challenges differ in many ways, both can be traced to the seventeenth century. Whatever one's view of the degree of cultural consensus characteristic of medieval Europe, it is clear that the social and political upheavals that followed the Reformation led to a profound reassessment of traditional practices, even as the nearly simultaneous encounters of Europeans with the indigenous peoples of Africa, Asia, and the Americas forced a rethinking of Western ideas of humanity, culture, and religion that continues to this day. Given its role in the violence that engulfed Europe throughout much of the seventeenth century and its overwhelmingly conservative response to new ways of understanding the world that were emerging at that time, the church's claims to authority came under particular scrutiny. Waves of skepticism regarding the significance of church teachings forced Christians to reconsider the basis on which they claimed to speak with authority.

A FAILED SOLUTION: THE DOCTRINE OF REVELATION

Appeal to divine revelation represents one strategy that Christians theologians have adopted to meet this challenge. This doctrine began to assume a specifically apologetic role in the wake of the Enlightenment, as theologians increasingly felt it necessary to preface their work with some preliminary justification of its intellectual validity. Under the general heading of theological prolegomena, discussion of revelation helped to dispose the reader favorably to subsequent doctrinal claims by defending both the meaningfulness and the distinctiveness of theological discourse in terms of broader philosophical and/or anthropological categories.[8] By the early nineteenth century, this apologetic thrust reached a certain climax in the work of Friedrich Schleiermacher, who argued in the second edition of his *The Christian Faith* that theological prolegomena needed to be free of any specifically Christian presuppositions if theology hoped to lay claim to intellectual respectability.[9]

While Schleiermacher's views have been challenged almost from the moment he formulated them, his position does illustrate the apologetic context within which the modern doctrine of revelation took shape. Honed in reaction to the combined influence of Descartes, Locke, and Kant (who together brought questions about the conditions of knowledge to the fore in Western philosophy), the doctrine of revelation stands as the product of theologians' struggles to defend the possibility of human knowledge of (and thus talk about) God. In this century, Karl Barth (probably the most influential critic of this approach to theology) specifically rejected Schleiermacher's claim that theological prolegomena should be free of specifically Christian content.[10] In his view, the importance of theological prolegomena has nothing to do with the contingent need to defend the faith in the face of modern skepticism. It is, rather, demanded by the logic of Christian faith itself, as that which is based in the confession of Jesus Christ as the revealed Word of God.[11]

Barth's explicitly dogmatic prolegomena stand as a daring attempt to turn the challenge of the Enlightenment back on itself, but even for Barth, the question of knowledge retains a certain priority. In his thought, the doctrine of revelation still serves as a means countering the charge that Christian speech lacks a firm epistemological foundation. This epistemological undercurrent is clearest in Barth's correlation of the concept of revelation with the doctrine of the Trinity in the first volume of his *Church Dogmatics*. There Barth argues that the trinitarian structure of God can be interpreted in terms of the process of revelation itself, insofar as the latter includes the distinct stages of revealer, revealed, and revelation. To be sure, Barth is careful to note that this logical insight is theologically barren unless interpreted through the history of Jesus Christ. But in light of this history, he asserts that "without God's being historically revealed [as the triune reality of Revealer, Revealed, and Revelation], revelation would not be revelation."[12] God's freedom remains the only basis for human knowledge of God, but the question of the conditions of the possibility of such knowledge is evidently important enough for Barth to risk obscuring his own insistence on the sufficiency of the biblical witness by suggesting that the dogma of the Trinity follows from the logic of revelation rather than the other way around.

In any case, while Barth is content to dismiss the apologetic use of revelation, more recent critics have charged that the doctrine as a whole is burdened by insuperable logical difficulties.[13] Ronald Thiemann offers a particularly good account of the problem. He argues that in order to make sense of Christian claims to know God, a doctrine of revelation must maintain both that there is essential continuity between knowledge of God and knowledge of other things (otherwise it would be misleading to use the term "knowledge" for both) and that knowledge of God is unique (since it is a fundamental Christian conviction that we know God only because God graciously chooses to reveal God's self to us).[14] Thiemann contends that the doctrine of revelation, as traditionally formulated, necessarily collapses under the weight of these two demands. As he sees it, conventional doctrines of revelation all share a view of knowledge that can be traced to the Enlightenment. This view can be summarized as follows: Data from the world encounter our cognitive faculties, where they are ordered and interpreted in terms of a particular conceptual frame. Data cannot be known in the absence of a conceptual frame, in the same way that it is impossible to make sense of the positions occupied by pieces on a chessboard unless one is familiar with the rules of chess. The frame makes knowledge possible by relating individual data to one another in order to form a coherent picture of the world.

While this model of how we come to know has proven very useful in many contexts, Thiemann points out that it does not go well with the concept of revelation. The whole point of the doctrine of revelation is to affirm that God is knowable. Now, according to the Enlightenment model of knowledge, if God is knowable, then God can be located within a conceptual frame. The problem is that proponents of the doctrine of revelation also want to affirm the Christian belief that God is the source of all that is and, therefore, prior to and independent of every conceptual frame. The dilemma could not be more serious: either human beings cannot know God, or the God they know lacks the quality of absolute prevenience with respect to human beings that is a defining feature of Christian belief. Thiemann concludes that the "modern epistemological doctrine of revelation must be adjudged a failure not because of inept execution or insufficient imagination on the part of its defenders, but because of the impossible demands of the project itself."[15]

Notwithstanding this conclusion, Thiemann remains convinced that it is vital for Christians to continue to affirm both the priority of God as the source of theological knowledge and the integrity of human beings as those who know.[16] In this context, he faults several theologians who attempt to dispense with the category of revelation altogether on the ground that they "fail to account both for God's *priority* and for his *relation* to our human framework of concepts and categories."[17] Thiemann thus applauds the theological instincts of the proponents of revelation, even though he believes they make a fatal mistake when they take their cue from philosophy and thus find themselves forced to conceive of divine prevenience in epistemological terms.[18]

Convinced that the Christian belief in God's prevenience requires some notion of revelation, Thiemann tries to reformulate the doctrine. He accepts the supposition that all claims to knowledge are made within the context of a larger conceptual frame. He also maintains that these conceptual frames are organized around certain basic or "background" beliefs. These beliefs provide the criteria for what count as valid—or even meaningful—arguments within a particular conceptual frame.[19] Thiemann then argues that the Enlightenment marks the onset of a time when God's priority no longer functions as a background belief within most people's working conceptual frames. Instead, the idea of divine prevenience has become "a dependent belief" that must be justified by appeal to other principles which now have the status of background beliefs in Western thought.[20] While most theologians have accepted this shift and developed their doctrines of revelation accordingly (with the lack of success noted above), Thiemann points out that modern background beliefs (precisely insofar as they are *background* beliefs) are in themselves no more self-evident than those of the Christian frame they have displaced. Therefore, instead of trying to justify Christian claims on terms set by philosophers, Thiemann proposes a descriptive theology that plots the internal relations between Christian beliefs in an effort to show how the Christian claim that God is both prior and related to all conceptual frames (including the Christian one) coheres with other specifically Christian beliefs.[21] In this way, he hopes to address the issues faced by post-Enlightenment doctrines of revelation without buying into their crippling procedural presuppositions.[22]

As noted above, the doctrine of revelation, as conventionally formulated, comes to grief because it is impossible to maintain simultaneously that human beings know God *and* that God is absolutely prevenient: unless human beings are somehow involved in the act of revelation, it is hard to make sense of the claim that God is known; but if revelation is incomplete apart from human involvement, then God's prevenience is compromised because divine action becomes dependent on human response. Thiemann argues that these difficulties dissolve when the gospel is viewed as promise, because the meaning of the word "promise" (unlike that of "know") actually implies the prevenience of the promiser, yet without compromising the integrity of the one to whom the promise is given.[23] A promise, defined as "an intentional speech-act by which the speaker assumes an obligation to perform some specified future act on behalf of the hearer," depends entirely on the initiative of the promiser.[24] It is true that "in order for the promise to be 'nondefective' the hearer must . . . acknowledge that this speech-act fulfills the conditions of promising. But that acknowledgment does not in any sense constitute the promise."[25] A promise is in this way like a personal check: the payee needs to endorse the check to receive the money, but even if the check were never cashed, it would be no less valid.

The difficulties that plague epistemological approaches to the doctrine of revelation thus seem capable of easy resolution simply by sticking to the conceptual frame of the Gospels (in which God's prevenience as the giver of a promise is assumed) rather than by trying to square this conceptual frame with a competing one (in which God's prevenience has the status of a dependent belief). Yet Thiemann's solution is only convincing if it is indeed the case that the gospel is best construed as promise. According to Thiemann, this promise is communicated through the biblical narrative, especially in the canonical Gospels.[26] While no particular logical problems are entailed by the claim that a narrative can communicate a promise,[27] it is by no means self-evident that the biblical narrative in particular does so. Thiemann therefore goes to some trouble to show that his reading of the Bible is plausible as well as logically possible. Without repeating his rather extended argument, I think it can be granted that he succeeds in showing that the Bible can plausibly be interpreted as "narrated promise." Furthermore (and in keeping with the demands of his descriptive approach to theology), Thiemann also points out that this interpretation of Scripture is consistent with the way Christians have in fact read the Bible throughout their history.[28]

The problem is that by referring to the history of Christian practice as support for his contention that the Bible is best read as narrated promise, Thiemann seems to assign a certain theological priority to the established practices of the Christian community— a move that would seem to contradict his insistence on the unconditional priority of God in Christian belief.[29] An obvious response to this critique is that the validity of Thiemann's argument does not depend on reference to communal practice. If it is the case that the Christian churches in general (not to mention Thiemann himself) read the Scriptures as narrated promise, then this reading is justified (or not) by reference to the texts themselves. From this perspective, Thiemann needlessly confuses the issue by referring to the history of Christian practice, because the real basis for his claims (as his own extensive exegesis of the Gospel of Matthew suggests) is the meaning of the biblical texts. If his interpretation of the gospel as promise is exegetically sound, then his defense of divine prevenience works; if it is not, then his defense fails. The hermeneutical conventions of particular Christian communities have no bearing on the matter.

Unfortunately, this line of argument, far from strengthening Thiemann's position, actually undercuts it. The appeal of Thiemann's refusal to follow more-traditional approaches to the doctrine of revelation rests largely on his rejection of the presupposition that philosophy (or, for that matter, any other discipline) can provide an objective, univocal set of criteria in terms of which human judgments (theological or otherwise) can be evaluated. On the contrary, it is Thiemann's contention that *any* conceptual frame—that of various post-Enlightenment philosophies included—depends on certain (largely unquestioned) background beliefs that set the terms of "reasonableness" for that frame. Belief in God's prevenience functions as one such belief for Christians, but not for contemporary Western culture as a whole. As Thiemann puts it:

> Since belief in human dependence upon God's grace
> no longer functions as a culturally shared assumption, the-
> ologians have taken that fact either as a cue to start the
> apologetic engines in defense of revelation or as an indica-
> tion that Christians too must abandon that belief. Both
> alternatives are wrong-headed, because both allow the cul-
> tural situation to determine the logic of Christian belief. . . .
> I want to argue that theologians ought to reestablish
> theological consensus concerning prevenience, despite the
> irremediable lack of cultural consensus.[30]

Thiemann makes use of biblical exegesis as a means of reestablishing this theological consensus, but what he seems to overlook is that the persuasiveness of his exegesis is inseparable from the fact that he reads the Bible as a Christian, and thus from within a communally shaped conceptual frame. Biblical interpretation, after all, is itself a form of argument, and on Thiemann's own terms, any form of argument presupposes certain background beliefs. The fact that the issue of God's prevenience is itself a background belief does not make the arguments marshaled in support of it any less frame-dependent. It simply means that within the adopted conceptual frame, reasoning proceeds backward from widely accepted dependent beliefs to the background beliefs that they presuppose.[31]

The fact that Thiemann's arguments for divine prevenience are, on his own terms, necessarily frame-dependent renders his task of rehabilitating the doctrine of revelation problematic. Once again, the difficulty is that of reconciling the apparently irreconcilable demands that a viable Christian theology affirm both divine priority and human agency. On one hand, the category of narrated promise does appear to provide a means of affirming both propositions that is immeasurably simpler and more persuasive than the various approaches that take religious epistemology as their point of departure. On the other hand, this solution only pushes the problem back a step, because it depends on a particular community's way of reading the Bible and thus implicitly compromises divine prevenience by granting priority to human tradition. Thiemann makes a strong case that traditional formulations of the doctrine of revelation are unable to maintain a proper distinction between divine action and human response. But if the narrated promise that defines the gospel is accessible only by way of the community's hermeneutical conventions, how does his own reformulation of the doctrine avoid this same charge? Thiemann responds by claiming that Scripture constitutes an exception to the rule that context controls the interpretation of texts, arguing that "the structure and content of these [biblical] texts suggest a reverse hermeneutical procedure for their interpretation."[32] Nonetheless, it is hard to see how this defense can avoid the charge of question-begging. Thiemann does a credible job of showing that the Bible *can* be read as promise. However, in the absence of any further justification, this "can" raises an important question: once Christians become aware that the text can *also* be read in other ways (for example, historically-critically, psychoanalytically, or as preliminary to the definitive revelation of the Qur'an), how do they answer the charge that they themselves are the makers of the promises they attribute to God?

Notwithstanding these difficulties, Thiemann's descriptive approach to theology remains promising in the face of competing claims to authority mounted by other religions, philosophy, and the natural and social sciences. Refraining from the temptation of trying to demonstrate the compatibility of Christian claims with non-Christian conceptual schemes, he aims only to articulate the internal logic of Christian faith and practice. While his solution does succeed in showing that Christianity's claims are at least no more unreasonable than those of its competitors, there remains the nagging question of whether Thiemann's unavoidable (if largely implicit) appeal to the brute fact of ecclesial convention is satisfactory on Christianity's own terms, or whether it subverts the very claim to divine prevenience that Thiemann himself is so intent on preserving.

Of course, Thiemann's approach does not even begin to address the challenge to Christian claims to authority that comes from the poor and oppressed. Even if it is granted that Christians are no less justified in claiming authority for their pronouncements than anyone else, is that enough? Those concerned with issues of liberation would doubtless want to press the issue of why *any* claims to authority should be entertained, especially those of Christianity, given its history of association with (not to mention direct promotion of) the suppression of competing claims both within and without the confines of confessionally "Christian" cultures. Thiemann's account assumes a free market of conceptual frames in which no one is more privileged than any other, but even a cursory look at history suggests that the fates of conceptual frames are closely intertwined with the realities of political power. An adequate account of the Christian faith would therefore appear bound to ask how Christians should understand the connections between theology and politics.

chapter two

THE CHURCH'S AUTHORITY AND CHRIST'S AUTHORITY

Rejection of a doctrine of revelation beholden to the demands of philosophical epistemology has been shown as promising. An apologetic appeal to revelation as a means of securing the authority of Christian claims founders due to the impossibility of squaring the claim that God is the unique and sufficient source of revealed knowledge with the idea that knowledge is a genuinely human act. Because our knowing something is a function of our capacity to locate it within a larger conceptual frame, it is a contradiction in terms to maintain both that God is known through revelation *and* that this knowledge is independent of any reference to a conceptual frame.

In the face of these difficulties, Ronald Thiemann, as we saw, rejects as misguided the attempt to defend Christian belief in divine priority in non-Christian terms. Instead, he opts for the less ambitious task of describing the logic of Christian claims about the relationship between God and humankind. The persuasiveness of the description he offers, however, depends on the proposition that the biblical witness is best understood as an example of "narrated promise." Although he recognizes that this conclusion is consistent with the history of Christian interpretation of Scripture, Thiemann's concern to protect the principle of divine priority leads him to reject the idea that his conclusions are a function of his own commitment to a specifically Christian conceptual frame. Even though it means contradicting his own principle that all claims to knowledge are relative to the particular conceptual frame within which they are made, Thiemann resorts to the rather desperate claim that his reading of Scripture is simply the most natural one.

CHRISTOCENTRIC AND ECCLESIOCENTRIC DIMENSIONS

Thiemann's reluctance to follow through on the implications of his reasoning is understandable. Once the reading of Scripture as God's promise is recognized to be a function of specifically Christian hermeneutical practices, then all the logical difficulties associated with Christian belief in divine priority resurface. It may well be the case, as Thiemann argues, that the idea of promising implies prevenience; but if (as his own line of argument suggests) the fact that we interpret the gospel as promise in the first place depends on a prior commitment to a whole complex of community-specific practices, then appeal to Scripture is not by itself a sufficient ground for affirming God's prevenience with respect to the community. So long as God's identity as promiser is a function of communal practice, then it is impossible to know whether God is in fact the source of the gospel promise or whether Christians are simply the deluded manufacturers of their own consolation.

Even with its shortcomings, however, Thiemann's analysis brings into relief a basic difficulty accompanying any attempt to define the source and norm of Christian theological statements. On one hand, insofar as theology is understood as reflection on Christian faith and practice, its starting point is necessarily the concrete reality of the church. Through its characteristic patterns of speech and action, developed through the complex of interrelated activities that includes worship, the reading of Scripture, and the interpretation of events and movements in the world at large, the church provides the context within which a particular instance of discourse can be identified as Christian in the first place. Because there is no Christian theology except where people bother to identify themselves as Christians, any Christian theology is necessarily "ecclesiocentric," in the sense that the sociological fact of the church communities is both the occasion for and the immediate object of theological reflection.

On the other hand, it is one of the few truly common features of Christian churches that they do not regard whatever authority they claim as self-constituting, but trace it to Jesus of Nazareth, who, as the Christ, is understood to be the agent and bearer of God's rule in the world. To the extent that the mission and ministry of this figure are regarded as the source and norm of the practices that define a community as church, any purportedly Christian teaching must be tested against its conformity to the good news announced by Jesus. From this perspective, it follows that every theology that bothers to identify itself as Christian at all will look to the person of Jesus as its ground and therefore strive to be "Christocentric."

While Thiemann's interpretation of the biblical story of Jesus as a promise is consistent with a broad spectrum of established Christian practice, his account fails to stress the degree to which Christian talk about Jesus Christ is mediated by the sociological reality of the church. It is all very well to appeal to Scripture as the source and norm of what Christians say about Jesus, but the fact remains that the shape of any appeal to Scripture is bound up with the hermeneutical conventions of a particular community of faith. It follows that no specifically theological discussion of the biblical witness to Jesus is plausible unless it reckons explicitly with the church's role in shaping the content of Christian belief. From what has been said so far, it may be expected that this role will be somewhat peculiar; for insofar as Christian theology takes the form of an ecclesiocentric practice that claims a uniquely Christocentric content, the church would appear to be a community characterized by the ongoing critique of its own practices in the name of the priority of God in Jesus Christ.

In light of the interrelated facts that (1) Christian theological reflection is structured by the existence of communities that call themselves churches and (2) these communities understand their authority to be completely subject to the person of Jesus Christ, it seems reasonable to conclude that a coherent Christian theology will include both an ecclesiocentric and a Christocentric dimension. While the latter follows from Christian conviction regarding the logical priority of Christ over the church's practices, the former emphasizes the role of the church as the context within which talk of Christ assumes specifically Christian form. While Christians have almost always recognized the significance of both these dimensions for doing theology, a certain tension between them has been experienced regularly in church history. For example, the ecclesiocentric perspective has been invoked to check criticism of existing church practice in recognition of the community's role as the arbiter of specifically Christian discourse. Advocates of a more Christocentric point of view, on the other hand, have been inclined to stress that Jesus stands over against every community, regardless of its professedly Christian identity.

The course of these debates over the proper character of Christian discourse has varied enormously, resulting in a number of ecclesiastically distinct bodies, all claiming the title of "church." This proliferation of Christian communities led early on to the widely shared conclusion that not every group claiming ecclesial status should in fact be counted part of the church of Jesus Christ. Traditionally, these criteria of exclusion are divided into two basic categories, heresy and schism, which can be correlated with what I have called the Christocentric and ecclesiocentric dimensions of theology, respectively. Heresy is a matter of false teaching and, therefore, can generally be understood as error regarding the community's official teaching about Christ. Schism, on the other hand, involves breaking communal bonds with the larger faith community. While it need not involve doctrinal error, schism does place the schismatic outside the established communal context which defines faith and practice as specifically catholic (and, therefore, genuinely Christian).[1] As summarized by Augustine, if heresy is a violation of faith, schism transgresses against the demands of love.[2]

If the accusation of heresy is bound up with a perceived failure to make Christ the measure of Christian proclamation, the schismatic stands accused of having failed to recognize the church as the necessary context (or conceptual frame) for Christian faith and practice. In this way, it is possible (at least from the point of view of those levying the accusations) to speak of heresy as the attempt to have a church apart from Christ, while viewing schism as rooted in the presupposition that it is possible to encounter Christ outside of the church. Important though this distinction may be in theory, however, it has often proved extremely difficult to maintain in practice. Although schism has to do specifically with one's relationship to the church as an institution, it is generally open to being interpreted as a matter of doctrinal disagreement, often with particular reference to those doctrines that define the church as an institution.[3] It is therefore not surprising that in the history of the Christian churches, agreement in doctrine (orthodoxy) generally has been regarded as a sufficient measure of a community's membership in the wider church. While the content of orthodox teaching at virtually every crucial point in church history has been a matter of debate, the idea that doctrinal orthodoxy is the best criterion of ecclesial identity has proven to be a matter of broad consensus across denominational lines.[4]

Especially in this century, however, serious questions have been raised about the sufficiency of doctrine as an identifying mark of the church. This is certainly not to suggest that previous generations of Christians were unaware that doctrine alone might prove a less than adequate measure of faith. Luther, for example, understood the ease with which doctrine, treated as a fixed datum to be learned and repeated without reference to the ongoing life of the church, could become a dead letter:

> For everyone who travels, what he has left behind and forgotten is the letter, and what he is reaching forward to is the Spirit. For what one already possesses is always the letter, by comparison with what has to be achieved. . . . Thus the doctrine of the Trinity, when it was explicitly formulated at the time of Arius, was the Spirit, and only understood by a few; but today it is the letter, because it is something publicly known— unless we add something to it, i.e., a living faith in it.[5]

Insofar as orthodoxy is decided by agreement on the letter of doctrine, it is an inadequate measure of what Luther calls a "living faith." Without presuming to give a complete definition of this latter phrase, it seems at the very least to entail an active engagement with content of doctrine through participation in the day-to-day life of the church. This ongoing need for engagement is rooted in the fact that doctrine is formulated in the first place as the church, reflecting on the implications of its commitment to Jesus Christ, seeks to define for itself the content of that commitment in the face of various alternatives. Once a doctrine is widely accepted, however, the circumstances under which it was formulated are, as Luther notes, likely to be forgotten. The doctrine then becomes a dead letter with the result that the community's reliance on it as a means of self-definition may actually serve to impede its engagement with Jesus Christ. This outcome can be expected whenever assent to doctrine comes to be treated as the substance of faith rather than a mode by which faith is best expressed in a given situation. Accordingly (and somewhat paradoxically), we may restate Luther's point as follows: the greater the success of a doctrine, the greater the risk it poses to the life of the church.

From this insight it is a short but crucial step to the idea that a church's doctrine might be fully orthodox and still fail to communicate the gospel. Dietrich Bonhoeffer attacked the Lutheran church in Germany in just these terms.[6] Following Luther's idea that orthodox doctrine needs to be supplemented by a "living faith" to be theologically productive (or, better, to be kept from becoming theologically harmful), Bonhoeffer identified obedience as a defining feature of such faith. While this claim may appear to contradict Luther's insistence on justification by faith alone rather than works of obedience, Bonhoeffer countered that the Protestant establishment had bowdlerized Luther's teaching on justification by failing to recognize the importance of obedience for the Christian life.[7] For while Bonhoeffer accepted the proposition that we are justified by faith alone, he also insisted that faith in Christ was inseparable from obedience to Christ, because "only he who is obedient can believe."[8]

Such a close correlation between faith and obedience implies that a disobedient church loses its claim to be the church of Jesus Christ. Nor is disobedience simply a matter of failing to put Christian teaching into practice, as though the life of faith were a two-step process in which dogmatic propositions function as an ethical blueprint that precedes the concrete work of obedience. The point is rather that the meaning of doctrinal propositions themselves (and, therefore, the possibility of assent to them) is inseparable from the wider context of communal practices within which they originate. When the patterns of behavior in relation to which particular doctrines were formulated in the first place change, it is only natural that the doctrines themselves will acquire a different sense. One may make an analogy with board games: within the larger set of practices that define the game of chess, the meaning of the term "king" is clear, but statements about the role and significance of the king that are self-evident to the chess player will be unintelligible if transferred to the realm of checkers. In the same way, a church that is disobedient necessarily proclaims a different doctrine than an obedient church, precisely because it is disobedient, and thus plays by a different set of rules.

It is in this context that the ecclesiocentric dimension of theology is most critical. Doctrines that are widely accepted as orthodox admit of quite different meanings depending on the larger systems of practice within which they are situated. The biblical account of Peter at Caesarea Philippi (Matt. 16:13–23 and pars.) is a case in point. While Peter's profession of faith in Jesus as the Christ is impeccable from a doctrinal point of view, his inability to accept that the Christ "must suffer many things at the hands of the elders and the chief priests and scribes, and be put to death" shows how little he understands what this title means when applied to Jesus. Such understanding comes only in the actual course of taking up the cross and following Jesus (Matt. 16:24–25). Once again, this is not merely a question of putting Jesus' teaching into practice; it is rather a condition for understanding his teaching in the first place. Where the commitment to follow is lacking, the meaning of the words is divorced from its origin in the life of Jesus and shaped instead by the individual's own prejudices.

An even more pointed example of the role of context in shaping meaning is provided by the story of the rich young man (Mark 10:17–22 and pars.). Once again, there is nothing wrong with the protagonist's grasp of doctrine: the young man knows the commandments and, what is more, follows them (v. 20). The catch comes when he is faced with Jesus' further command to sell his possessions and give the proceeds to the poor. His withdrawal from the scene at this point certainly signifies a failure of obedience; yet it would be unfair to interpret this reaction as a simple matter of hypocrisy. As Bonhoeffer perceived, the young man's problem is not insincerity, but the fact that he has separated his knowledge *of* God's word from personal engagement *with* it.[9] The word has become a third thing interposed between himself and God instead of being recognized as God's own presence.[10] The young man's problem is therefore not that he disobeys the Ten Commandments or even that he disobeys Jesus' particular command, considered in the abstract. It is rather that he regards doctrine—including the commandments he so conscientiously keeps—as a self-contained reality, the content of which is independent of the lived context within which it is professed.

In the case of the rich young man no less than that of Peter, the biblical witness is clear: orthodoxy with respect to doctrine—and even obedience with respect to the commandments—is at best incomplete and at worst positively misleading apart from its integration into a broader context of behavior. The meaning of doctrine—even orthodox doctrine—is not constituted solely by a particular sequence of words; it is also a function of the situation within which those words are spoken and heard. Nor is this broader context, as depicted in Scripture, amorphous or merely ideal; on the contrary, it is constituted by the concrete reality of the person Jesus of Nazareth. Terms like "faith," "love," "covenant," and "salvation" acquire their proper meaning only in connection with this person. Likewise, it is only in encounter with Jesus that genuine obedience to the commandments is possible. It follows that even the most orthodox of words and lawful of actions lose the capacity to communicate the truth when they are separated from the one whose presence gives them their distinctively Christian meaning.

This interdependence of meaning and context suggests that orthodoxy is by itself an inadequate measure of Christian identity. Attention to the total life situation of the speaker is necessary not merely (or even primarily) as a test of the sincerity of one's doctrinal commitments, but also as a condition of determining what the doctrine in question in fact means. In this context, even Bonhoeffer's insistence on the need for obedience stands in need of further clarification. For while the category of obedience does point to the concrete demands of Christian faith, it also carries the connotation of a one-to-one correspondence between precept and fulfillment that, as shown by the story of the rich young man, can in its own way be just as far removed as a sterile orthodoxy from the life of discipleship. In this context, the neologism "orthopraxy," understood to refer to the whole complex of actions that give Christian doctrines their force as testimony to the presence of Jesus Christ, may prove a better terminological complement to "orthodoxy."

Perhaps no movement within the church has reflected more extensively on the requirements of orthopraxy than the various theologies of liberation. Despite frequent caricatures to the contrary, liberation theologians are generally quite careful to distinguish their emphasis on praxis from a doctrine of works righteousness. And despite the importance these theologians attribute to the realization of human freedom in history, their focus on praxis is less soteriological than ecclesiological in nature. In other words, orthopraxy does not function as a direct measure of the individual's status before God (soteriology), but rather as a touchstone against which to measure particular communities' claims to be the church (ecclesiology).

Because orthopraxy, unlike schism, cannot be determined simply by reference to membership in a particular church, it is better able to hold its own as an ecclesiological criterion alongside orthodoxy. Its use as such a criterion has the effect of bringing the tension between the ecclesiocentric and Christocentric dimensions of theological reflection into relief. This is particularly evident in the way that the liberationist refuses to yield before theological judgments not born out of the experience of the community. Yet while the whole idea of liberation theology has been criticized for being too ecclesiocentric, the charge that it amounts to a betrayal of the priority of Jesus Christ fails to take into account the possibility that the focus on the community which is characteristic of liberation theology may be justified on Christological grounds. This possibility has been defended with particular force by James Cone in the context of his efforts to develop a black theology of liberation: "We must say unequivocally that who Jesus Christ is for black people today is found through an encounter with him in the social context of black existence. But as soon as that point is made, the other side of the paradox must be affirmed; otherwise the truth of black experience is distorted. The Jesus of black experience is the Jesus of Scripture."[11] That is, only by virtue of the specific content of the New Testament witness to Jesus of Nazareth can the experience of the black community serve as a criterion for the evaluation of Christian faith and practice.[12]

The particular conditions that render the social context of the African American (or any other) church decisive for Christian reflection on Jesus are discussed below. For the time being, it is sufficient to note that by coordinating rather than opposing the ecclesiocentric and Christocentric dimensions of theology, liberation theologians like Cone raise the possibility that the tension between them might prove theologically productive. Obviously, this possibility stands or falls with being able to interpret the church's mediation of encounter with Jesus as more than a regrettable feature of the "ugly ditch" of history that separates us from the first century. Instead, Jesus' presence in and through the church must be shown to be a defining feature of his sovereignty. And while in many respects this conviction underlies any Christian community's claim to speak with Jesus' authority, the liberationist stress on orthopraxy means that Christ's presence in the community cannot be assumed, even where a community's doctrine is impeccably orthodox. On the contrary, the insights of liberation theology suggest that it is precisely the community whose own identity as a church is most questioned by the arbiters of orthodoxy that may prove the most suitable vehicle for manifesting God's presence in the world.

CHRIST AND CONTEXT

In this respect, it is not simply fortuitous that black theology should serve as the occasion for reflection on this topic. Few peoples have had their identity as a people subject to the degree of systematic assault as have Americans of African descent. Forcibly removed from their native land, African American slaves were deliberately separated from others who shared their language and culture in order to undermine the possibility of their organized resistance to enslavement. While the degree to which traces of the slaves' African heritage survived this assault remains a subject of debate within scholarly circles,[13] there is no question that the effect of the slave system on the cultural heritage of African Americans was catastrophic.

That this violence was perpetrated on African Americans by Christians and, indeed, defended as a means of "Christianizing" them is graphic proof of the potentially demonic character of orthodoxy when separated from orthopraxy. Of course, it is true that the doctrine of those who evangelized the slaves could also be (and often enough was) defective. While the particular conditions of slave catechesis varied somewhat with time period, geographical region, and social context (for example, large plantations versus smaller farms or towns), the "gospel" the slaves were preached frequently had little to do with the good news of Jesus Christ. And yet, arguably, the failure of white Christians was finally less a matter of overt doctrinal error than of faulty praxis fostered by the wholesale subordination of Scripture to the interests of maintaining the social order of the old South.

In the theology that emerged from this process, any suggestion that Christianity was inconsistent with slavery or the racist ideology that supported it was rigorously suppressed. Indeed, in some cases, nervous pastors made it a condition of baptism that slaves swear an oath to the effect that they did not accept the faith with the hope or understanding that it would effect any change in their civil status.[14] Laws were passed throughout the South forbidding slaves from acquiring the literacy skills that would have allowed them to check what they were taught against the witness of Scripture. That slaves continued to claim Christianity as their own under such conditions is as remarkable as it is undeniable. Nor can slave Christianity simply be dismissed as an ideology of submission and otherworldly compensation. While the precise numbers involved will never be known, it is clear that considerable numbers of slaves weaned themselves of their owners' interpretations of the Christian faith in favor of the very different gospel of their own "brush arbor" meetings, normally convened at night and in secret in order to evade the master's eye.[15] These meetings were often announced in the fields through the call-and-response singing of the spirituals, whose otherworldly surface vocabulary concealed from suspicious ears a very real engagement with issues of dignity and freedom in this life.[16]

While the kind of organized, militant resistance to slavery visible in the revolts of Denmark Vesey and Nat Turner (or, in different form, in Harriet Tubman's Underground Railroad) was comparatively rare,[17] slaves had other means of critiquing the version of the gospel sanctioned by their masters. Consider the reaction experienced by the Reverend Charles Colcock Jones, one of the most prominent white missionaries to slaves in the antebellum South, when he preached a more or less standard sermon warning slaves not to attempt escape:

> The effect of his admonishments, according to Jones, is that half of his audience walked off and those remaining looked dissatisfied. Jones shares that the remaining slaves expressed their anger at the close of the service with tremendous vehemence by telling him that there was no such gospel in the Bible or that his sermon was not the gospel. Others took the bold track of telling him that he was preaching to please the masters and that they would not return to hear any more of his preaching.[18]

This sort of critique of the standard "slaves-obey-your-masters" homily was by no means atypical.[19] In evaluating its merits, however, it is necessary to recognize that Jones's message is not without biblical warrant (see, for example, 1 Cor. 7:20–21; Eph. 6:5–6; Col. 4:22; Philem. 12). Nor can the content of his sermon simply be dismissed as a sycophantic capitulation to the interests of the slaveowners.[20] All the same, the objections brought by the slaves are decisive: whatever the accuracy of his scriptural citation and however unimpeachable his motives, the circumstances of Jones's address undermined completely his claim to be preaching the good news of Jesus Christ. However orthodox his doctrine, the context within which it was spoken effectively blocked Jones's stated aim of communicating the gospel.

The question that comes immediately to mind is where the slaves acquired the theological leverage to reject Jones's doctrine.

One way to answer this question is to take seriously the idea that the meaning of doctrine is inseparable from the context within which it is learned and repeated. In the biblical temptation narratives, for example, Jesus rejects the devil's appeals on the grounds that they represent a misapplication (and, therefore, a fundamental misapprehension) of biblical texts (Matt. 4:1–11; Luke 4:1–13). The slaves' rejection of proslavery theology can be interpreted in the same vein, as a matter of identifying the context within which a biblical text functions as gospel. For the New Testament writers, the determinative factor in shaping the evangelical character of any sequence of words is quite simply the presence of Jesus Christ. It is, in other words, only in the context of their day-to-day encounters with Jesus that the disciples discover the meaning of terms like "Christ," "realm," "greatness," and "God"—meanings that often run against their own theological sensibilities.[21] Likewise, the slaves' critique of the version of Christianity propounded by Jones and his colleagues was based on the recognition that it was just not consistent with the reality of Jesus of Nazareth.

To be sure, the slaves did not encounter Jesus in just the same way as the disciples did: as a human being under the conditions of time and space. All the same, that the slave experience of Jesus was one of genuine encounter (and not simply historical reconstruction) is implicit in their conviction that "a little talk with Jesus makes it right." The slaves knew Jesus as one who was present, to whom the believer could "steal away" in prayer. But—and this point is crucial if the "otherworldly" caricature of slave religion is to be countered effectively—the Jesus of the slave experience was not an idol of private consolation. On the contrary, the individual's ability to encounter Jesus in moments of solitude was firmly predicated on the prior experience of Jesus' presence in the community. The structure of slave belief (subject to attack on all sides by suspicious whites) was thoroughly bound up with the ability of individual slaves to regard themselves as part of a trustworthy community defined by mutual solidarity in a situation of poverty and oppression.

The spirituals in particular lend support to the idea that the slaves' encounter with Jesus was mediated through their understanding of themselves as a people. On a purely formal level, the call-and-response style of spiritual singing is indicative of the dialogical form of slave reflection on the faith. The communal character of slave religion is further suggested by the thematic content of the spirituals. Unlike many European and white American hymns of the same era, songs like "Go Down, Moses," "Oh Mary, Don't You Weep," and "Didn't My Lord Deliver Daniel?" place the slaves' encounter with God in the context of encounter with one another rather than in that of the individual soul's private pilgrimage to God. This same communal emphasis continues to mark formal worship in black congregations, where it is customary for the preacher to interrupt his or her sermon (thereby implicitly opening its content to question) in order to ask the congregation to witness to God's presence.[22]

The idea that a living encounter with Jesus constitutes the necessary setting for Christian faith and practice is, of course, not original with the African American religious experience. But the extreme circumstances under which this insight was appropriated by American slaves give their story supreme significance for American Christianity. The fact that slaves experienced Jesus as the one source of hope and dignity in a world that actively sought to deprive them of both was intimately bound up with a recognition that Jesus' presence could not simply be taken for granted as a corollary of correct doctrine. On the contrary, the value of doctrine was understood to be entirely dependent on one's encountering Jesus—the possibility of which was understood to require a physical commitment to the life of a community no less than an intellectual commitment to a given set of beliefs.

THE QUESTIONABLE CHARACTER OF THE COMMUNITY

To recognize that the meaning of doctrine (and, therefore, the content of belief) is inseparable from the character of the community within which those doctrines are professed says nothing about how the merits of any particular community are to be evaluated. The slaves' rejection of the stock sermons preached by proslavery ministers may seem eminently justified from the distance of nearly a century and a half, but it is important to be able to give reasons for this judgment if it is to be claimed as something more than a matter of contemporary prejudice. Special care should be taken to avoid romantic characterizations of slave religion as some sort of ideal manifestation of Christian faith. On the contrary, the irregular character of slave catechesis virtually guaranteed that the lines between orthodox Christian belief and folk traditions preserved from Africa or adopted from American Indian and European cultures would remain fluid. The slave narratives bear witness that the faith that emerged from the intersection of so many cultural forces was a highly syncretistic one, in which the rituals associated with the practices collectively known as "conjure" often commanded as much respect (not least for their role in cultivating resistance to slavery) as those of Christianity. In light of the breadth of religious and cultural symbolism appropriated by African Americans as part of their strategy of survival under extraordinarily difficult conditions, Gayraud Wilmore has gone so far as to suggest that slave religion is properly characterized as only more or less Christian.[23]

Clearly, if the assurance of survival were the only criterion of slave religion, the tension between the Christocentric and ecclesiocentric dimensions of theology would evaporate and the experience of the community would simply trump all other theological considerations. However things may have stood with the slaves, some contemporary black theologians can seem to embrace just this position. James Cone, for example, makes a point of arguing that the priority of Christ must be denied to the extent that it is equated with the priority of the doctrinal and ecclesiological categories of white Christians: "It is asked whether the black experience exists independently of Jesus Christ. If by Jesus Christ is meant the formal preaching and teaching of white missionaries, at a particular point in time, then the answer is an unqualified Yes. . . . But if by Jesus Christ is meant 'the image of the invisible God' . . . then the answer is an unqualified No."[24] Only on these terms does Cone presume to affirm "the interdependence of Jesus and the black experience."[25] But on these terms he does affirm it fully. Although Cone defends the logical priority of Jesus with respect to black experience,[26] he insists that Jesus' identity is inseparable from that experience because Jesus' own life was defined by solidarity with the oppressed. It is thus Cone's contention "that the God who was revealed in the life of oppressed Israel and who came to us in the incarnate Christ and who is present today as the Holy Spirit has made a decision about the black condition. God has chosen to make the black condition *God's* condition."[27]

Jesus is, according to Cone, both manifest in and the basis of the experience of black Americans. As extreme as this position may appear, however, in the final analysis, Cone's understanding of the relationship between Jesus and black experience does not simply erase the Christocentric side of the theological equation. Cone does not invoke "experience" as an independent factor alongside Scripture (as though the community were somehow independent of Christ), but rather as a theological category derived from Scripture's portrayal of the relationship between the God of Scripture and the community.[28]

As already noted, an ecclesiocentric approach to theology carries with it the risk that Christians will be led to identify their own speech with God's, thereby transforming theology into an all-too-easy exercise in self-justification. Cone in particular has been accused of succumbing to this risk, but even a cursory reading of his work makes it clear that self-justification is hardly what he has in mind. On the contrary, his whole theology is an insistent critique of the self-justifying character of white theology—a trait he attributes to the failure of European and white American theologians to reckon with the degree to which their own perspectives are marked by the experience of their communities.[29] The point of this critique is not to accuse one theology of being more ecclesiocentric than the other but to point out that black theology acknowledges its ecclesiocentric character in a way that white academic theology generally does not.

In this context, Cone's enthusiasm for the particularity of black theology should not be viewed as vulgar parochialism, for he is fully aware of the dangers that follow when a community absolutizes its own theological perspective. But he attacks the issue in a new way. The problem with a one-sidedly ecclesiocentric theology is that it leaves no space from which it is possible to stand over against the community in order to critique its practices in the name of Jesus Christ. Faced with this dilemma, white theology has generally been preoccupied with trying to minimize the epistemological interference generated by the community. As Cone and other liberation theologians argue, however, these attempts at objectivity not only have proven self-deceptive, but also (and for that very reason) have had the effect of silencing the voices of white women and people of color. Traditional theology stumbles because it is unable to see any alternative between a false universalism (in which the theological significance of the church is minimized) and a narrow parochialism (in which the present shape of communal practice is viewed as the final measure of theological truth). Liberation theologians like Cone strive to get beyond this apparent impasse by refusing to speak of "the church" as a monolithic or uniform entity that either acts or can be adequately analyzed as a bloc. Instead, the church is viewed as a social structure marked by the same sorts of internal differentiation characteristic as human communities in general.

Chief among these structures is the distinction between those who have power in the community and those who do not. By highlighting these intracommunal distinctions, Cone, along with other liberation theologians, calls into question the (often implicit) practice of identifying the church as a whole with its constituted authorities. From the perspective of *Realpolitik* as well as of practical sociology, it is no doubt understandable that those whose "official" positions of leadership allow them to select and enforce membership criteria should define the essence of a community. Cone, however, argues that this process is completely unjustified when it comes to a theological analysis of the church. He bases this claim on the observation that God in Jesus Christ identified with Israel's least rather than its leaders, thereby disclosing a gap between the covenant community's sociological and theological centers of gravity. This gap provides the leverage Cone and other liberation theologians need to give their ecclesiocentric approaches a critical edge. Recognition of the way in which different sociological contexts shape the theological perspectives of the powerful and the powerless makes it possible both to insist that God always speaks *from within* the community (through the oppressed) and to maintain that God nonetheless stands *over against* the community (as defined institutionally by its leadership).

In the same way that Jesus spoke as a Jew, but from the margins of the established Palestinian Jewish community, so God's word to the church today is mediated through its most marginalized members. By arguing in this way, black and other liberation theologians are able to recognize the particularity of communal experience as an unavoidable component of theological reflection and thereby mount an effective critique of facile claims to universalism. At the same time, however, to the extent that the experience not of the community's leaders but of its politically least influential members is understood to be theologically significant, this focus on experience is kept from degenerating into an automatic endorsement of the ecclesiastical status quo.

This distinction between the oppressors and the oppressed is the basis for Cone's evaluation of other Christian theologies. Any theology that refuses to acknowledge the theological relevance of the speaker's social location he rejects out of hand for having failed to recognize the elementary point that "oppressed and oppressors cannot possibly mean the same thing when they speak about God."[30] To be sure, this focus on the oppressed carries its own risks: if only the powerless have claim to the name of Christian, then there seems no theological ground from which their own practice may be critiqued—let alone a means of determining who is to be numbered among the (now privileged) ranks of the oppressed. Yet the liberationist emphasis on the hermeneutical role of the oppressed does not entail a wholesale condemnation of mainstream theology. Despite his unrelenting critique of white theology, even Cone is not dismissive of the historical significance of white theology for the black churches in North America:

When Jesus spoke of the gospel as new wine, it did not mean a total rejection of Judaism. What he meant was that the revolutionary message could not be restricted to the possibilities available in the old [doctrinal and communal] structures.

Similarly, because our knowledge of Christianity came from white oppressors, the black theology view of God is in part dependent on white theologians, but this does not mean white theologians set the criteria for black theology. Liberation means that the oppressed must define the structure and scope of reality for themselves; they do not take their cues from oppressors.[31]

Cone has no interest in denying the links between the black church and white theology. What he rejects is the inference that this historical connection gives white Christians special critical purchase over the black church. Instead, he argues that Christ's identification with the oppressed means that white American Christians have nothing theologically significant to contribute to the faith of their African American counterparts so long as they cling to their sociologically privileged position.[32]

Therefore, although the established leadership may provide the subject matter for Christian theological reflection, it does not thereby constitute the church. The true church is rather the community that, in obedience to Jesus, "freely becomes oppressed, because they know that Christ himself has defined human liberation in the context of what happens to the little ones."[33]

This variety of ecclesiocentrism is notable for the fact that judgments regarding a community's status as church cannot be viewed as a matter of theological or institutional pedigree. In fact, Cone reverses conventional ecclesiological wisdom by arguing that the ecclesiastically questionable character of African American slaves and other oppressed Christian groups, far from compromising their theological significance, is its ground. This is certainly not to say that the oppressed are themselves the source of the gospel, let alone to imply that Cone regards every opinion expressed by a poor person as theologically valid simply by virtue of its origin. It does mean, however, that no theology can be judged adequate that does not arise out of a genuine encounter with the poor as those through whom the God of Jesus Christ both sustains and judges the church. Solidarity with the oppressed is thereby proposed as a necessary, if not sufficient, condition of faithful Christian talk about God.

Nonetheless, Cone's approach does leave certain questions open. Granted that the recognition of sociological differentiation between different groups within the church provides a logical mechanism for resolving the tension between the ecclesiocentric and Christocentric dimensions of theology, it still needs to be asked why the poor in particular should be regarded as the focus of God's activity in Jesus Christ. Liberation theologians in general and Cone in particular argue that the privileging of the poor is demanded by the scriptural witness to Jesus, but their own methodological insights seem to render this kind of claim problematic. On one hand is the rather obvious fact that the "preferential option for the poor" has not always been recognized as a central feature of the biblical narrative over the course of the church's history. On the other hand, the value of liberation theologians' own exegetical arguments seem compromised by their recognition that any reading of Scripture is bound up with the social location of the reader. To be sure, the idea that one's understanding of Scripture is a function of one's social location does not rule out the logical possibility that one interpretation may be superior to another, but it certainly does seem to relativize the force of any argument one might make in support of such a claim.

Cone himself explicitly eschews the ideal of dispassionate objectivity on the grounds that the truth of God is partisan,[34] but he does not absolve himself of the responsibility to give reasons for his beliefs. In light of the degree to which Cone's theology has developed in response to critiques made by black women in particular,[35] there is little basis for interpreting Cone's theological privileging of the oppressed as a means of excusing himself from intellectual accountability.[36] As Cone himself emphasizes, the point of making black experience the point of reference for theological reflection is not to silence competing claims to truth but simply to ensure that they are recognized *as* competing claims and not imposed on the African American community as self-evident or universal truths.

With regard to biblical interpretation in particular, the issue is therefore not whether blacks and other oppressed Christians ought to be able to defend their beliefs on the basis of Scripture, but rather the kind of defense they should be expected to give.

The liberationist recognition of the social component in any biblical interpretation reinforces Thiemann's contention that the goal of objective proof from self-evident premises is misguided, but (as Thiemann also notes) deductive proof is not the only mode of rationality. Though the approach to Scripture on which black theology is based is not the only possible one, it may still be the best hermeneutical option. The question is how such a judgment can be made, given that no defense of a community's herme-neutical practices can escape some degree of prior commitment to those practices.

If a liberationist hermeneutic of the kind employed by Cone is to be justified on its own terms, it is therefore necessary (1) to be able to derive the community's privileging of the oppressed from the biblical witness (thereby affirming the theological priority of the Christ, who is the object of that witness) while (2) taking into account the fact that the content of this witness is itself a function of the community's social practice (thereby recognizing the role of the church in mediating Christ to the world). Showing how these requirements can be met is the task of the next two chapters. First, the case will be made that the theological priority of Christ is realized precisely in the hermeneutical activation of the church. The argument will then identify the poor as that group within the church that constitutes the particular locus from which Christ both encounters and shapes the community as a whole.

chapter three

THE CHURCH'S AUTHORITY AND THE PRIORITY OF SCRIPTURE

African American slaves' reliance on their own communities of faith as the context for resisting the Christianity preached to them by their owners does not imply that they set the community over against Scripture as the definitive witness to Jesus Christ. After all, the slaves' reported disgust at the sermon preached by the Reverend Jones was not directed at the Bible; quite the contrary, it was their view that Jones had falsified the biblical witness. Nevertheless, the fact that the experience of the community (rather than explicit citation of chapter and verse) seems to function as the basis for this judgment raises questions about how the relationship between Christ and the church is to be understood. The urgency of this question is only magnified by the contention of contemporary black theologians that the experience of African Americans rightly functions as a criterion for the evaluation of doctrine in the present day.

SCRIPTURE AS THE POINT OF CONFLICT

Because black theologians like James Cone continue to insist that the practices of the black church derive from the person of Jesus the Christ, the controversy over the role of the community in black theology points to the broader question of the relationship between the ecclesiocentric context of Christian theology and its Christocentric ground. For while the confession of Christ's priority over the church is a characteristic feature of Christian communities, the way in which this priority is understood varies from community to community with respect to both the material question of which practices are viewed as the product of divine mandate,[1] and the formal question of the procedures to be followed in determining how such judgments are to be made.

The search for a way to ensure that the confession of Christ's priority is realized in ecclesiastical practice is as old as the church itself (see Acts 15:1–35), and has generated a number of proposals: adherence to the church's teaching office as guaranteed by the apostolic succession of bishops (among Catholics), the decrees of ecumenical councils as received by local communities (among the Orthodox churches), canonical Scripture (for the churches of the so-called magisterial Reformation), and apostolic practice (among the Anabaptists and some earlier ascetic movements) have all been offered as criteria of Christian faithfulness to Jesus Christ.

Without attempting to assess the relative merits of these different proposals, it can be said that all of them look to Scripture as the source of the complex of vocabulary and concepts that shape their understanding of the Christian story. What divides them is less their reverence for Scripture as the definitive witness to the person of Jesus Christ than their respective understandings of the way in which this witness is preserved within the community. The issue is therefore best viewed as a question of the relationship between the priority of the Christ witnessed to in Scripture and the life of the community as the place where that witness is mediated to the world at large. The Reformation principle of "Scripture alone," or *sola Scriptura,* is a particularly appropriate focus for reflection on this question since it allows for the sharpest possible opposition between the Christocentric ground of theology and its ecclesiocentric articulation.

The Reformers defended *sola Scriptura* as a challenge to Catholic emphasis on the importance of the church's teaching office in the correct interpretation of Scripture. Their argument was that to assign a central hermeneutical role to the community constituted a fatal confusion of the human with the divine and thus a compromise

41

of divine priority.[2] In short, the Reformers refused to concede that the meaning of Scripture was determined by its use within the community; on the contrary, they insisted that all communal practice was to be tested against Scripture. In the words of the Lutheran Formula of Concord: "We believe, teach, and confess that the prophetic and apostolic writings of the Old and the New Testaments are the only rule and norm according to which all doctrines and teachers alike must be appraised and judged. . . . Other writings of ancient and modern teachers, whatever their names, should not be put on a par with Holy Scriptures."[3]

Although neither Luther nor Calvin was inclined to underestimate the importance of the church for the life of faith, both insisted that Scripture stood over the church (whether understood in terms of magisterium, councils, or a charismatic assembly of saints) as the Word of God, upon which the church was utterly dependent and from which it was therefore absolutely distinct. For both of them, belief in divine priority demanded *sola Scriptura*.

Catholic reservations about the Scripture principle do not necessarily imply any less devotion to Scripture than that found among Protestants. Still, the two communions' different senses of the relationship between Scripture and the church have proved a lasting point of contention between them. Catholics have maintained that because Scripture is open to any number of readings, a specifically Christian interpretation must be guided by definite hermeneutical principles established within the believing community. These principles are held to be trustworthy by virtue of God's pledge of the Holy Spirit to the community.[4]

In this respect, the Catholic position has something in common with that of the radical Reformers, who also tended to view Scripture as a text whose meaning could be grasped only by reference to the established hermeneutical judgment of the community, as guaranteed by adherence to a certain polity or by the special illumination of the Holy Spirit.[5] Not that either Catholics or the various radical sects had any interest in calling divine priority into question, but neither were they inclined to allow that the established practice of the community of faith could be fundamentally opposed to God's Word. For Luther and Calvin, on the other hand, the principle of divine priority meant that the established practices of the community could be opposed to the will of God. Scripture was the only valid test of whether or not they were.

Sola Scriptura is therefore far more than an affirmation of biblical authority (which neither Catholics nor Anabaptists would be inclined to deny). Underlying the Scripture principle is the far more controversial claim that the determination of Scripture's meaning does not require reference to the church's established traditions of interpretation.[6] Therefore, while only the Holy Spirit can convince the reader that Scripture's witness is trustworthy, one cannot avoid confronting that witness on the grounds that its meaning is obscure.[7]

Luther sketched out the theological rationale for this position in his literary debate with Erasmus. Arguing that the church is commissioned to proclaim God's Word in Scripture as good news, and that this news can be the basis of faith only if there is no doubt as to its meaning, Luther concluded that a doctrine of scriptural clarity was implicit in the logic of Christian belief. To suggest otherwise would be to make Scripture an impediment rather than an aid to faith:

> And what is it that preachers do, to this very day? Do they interpret and expound the Scriptures? Yet if the Scripture they expound is uncertain, who can assure us that their exposition is certain? Another new exposition? And who will expound the exposition? At this rate we shall go on forever. In short, if Scripture is obscure or ambiguous, what point was there in God's giving it to us? Are we not obscure and ambiguous enough without having our obscurity, ambiguity, and darkness augmented for us from heaven? What, then, will become of that word of the apostle: "All Scripture inspired by God is profitable for teaching, for reproof, for correction"?[8]

This insistence on scriptural clarity is the cornerstone of Luther's Scripture principle (though, unlike later Protestant Scholastics, he felt no need to link it to a more elaborate theory of verbal inspiration or biblical inerrancy). For Luther, the clarity of Scripture was simply a necessary implication of the priority of God as reflected in the saving work of Jesus: God saves through the gospel of Jesus Christ; because human beings encounter the gospel through the preacher's exposition of Scripture, and because the good news of the gospel is precisely that the justifying grace of God in Jesus Christ does not depend on human ability (exegetical or otherwise), the clarity of Scripture must be affirmed.

This having been said, it would be entirely mistaken to conclude that the Reformers divorced Scripture from its use within the community of faith. For Luther in particular, the truth of Scripture was always a function of its being proclaimed.[9] The clarity upon which he insists is not to be understood as a property of the biblical texts taken in the abstract, but of Scripture as proclaimed and heard in the church:

> There is . . . an external judgment, whereby with the greatest
> certainty we judge the spirits and dogmas of all men, not
> only for ourselves, but also for others and for their salvation.
> This judgment belongs to the public ministry of the Word
> and to the outward office, and is chiefly the concern of lead-
> ers and preachers of the Word. We make use of it when we
> seek to strengthen those who are weak in faith and confute
> opponents. This is what we earlier called "the external clarity
> of Holy Scripture." Thus we say that all spirits are to be
> tested in the presence of the Church at the bar of Scripture.[10]

This external clarity of Scripture is less a statement about what Scripture is than about how it is to be used. Luther's point is not that anyone set down in front of a Bible will necessarily interpret it correctly. Scripture's clarity is rather a function of the public ministry of preaching within a community that understands the Bible as God's Word to and for it. In this context, to speak of Scripture's ambiguity is to have misunderstood its role as the source of the church's preaching. For Luther, the meaning of Scripture is clear not because it is some sort of magical, self-interpreting text, but simply because its witness is the substance and ground of Christian hope.

While the logic of Luther's position is compelling, the persistent lack of agreement among Christians regarding Scripture's meaning suggests that the relationship between Scripture and community cannot be resolved as easily as he seems to believe. To be sure, Luther nowhere claims that Scripture's clarity guarantees hermeneutical consensus among all who call themselves Christians.[11] As noted above, *sola Scriptura* is not a theory attributing special properties to the biblical texts but a statement about how Scripture is to be used in the church. Still, Luther does claim that the external clarity of Scripture means that "the spirits and dogmas" of all human beings can be judged "with the greatest certainty." This being the case, it does not seem unreasonable to ask how it is possible to decide between conflicting positions on the basis of Scripture when the meaning attributed to Scripture seems so closely tied to the ecclesial context within which it is expounded.

Reflecting on this question, Ernst Käsemann has concluded that the enormous theological diversity within the New Testament witness itself makes a direct appeal to Scripture very unstable ground on which to base the unity of the church.[12] But if the witness of Scripture can be cited in support of a number of different and mutually incompatible positions, on what basis are some interpretations to be rejected as false? Käsemann certainly has no interest in making the community the measure of correct interpretation; quite the contrary, he insists that "a congregation which calls itself Christian is devoid of any authority at all—indeed, must be called to order and repentance—when it makes itself the measure of the evangelical Word it is charged to utter."[13]

Yet this undeniable priority of the Word does not translate into the priority of Scripture. Invoking Paul's distinction between the spirit and the letter, Käsemann argues that the theologically varied texts that make up the biblical canon can only be interpreted correctly when read within the proper conceptual grid. According to Käsemann, this grid is defined by the Reformation doctrine of justification, which, he argues, ought to be made the touchstone of the church's reception of all tradition—including the tradition of Scripture.[14]

While Käsemann clearly addresses the questions left open in Luther's analysis of *sola Scriptura,* the solution he proposes surrenders the principle of scriptural clarity by conceding that Scripture's meaning is indeterminate apart from appeal to an existing tradition of interpretation. In this context, Gerhard Ebeling has noted that Käsemann's claims for the doctrine of justification bear a striking resemblance to Catholic insistence on coherence with church tradition as a criterion of correct biblical interpretation.[15]

Against this position, Ebeling argues that any appeal to a doctrinal "canon within the canon" betrays a fundamental misunderstanding of the Scripture principle. Briefly, if the content of Scripture is not sharply distinguished from any particular tradition of interpretation (including the tradition established by the Reformers) it cannot be defended as the Word of God.[16] Once again, the fundamental dilemma identified by Thiemann raises its head: if the content of revelation (here identified with Scripture) is made dependent on some human trait (like tradition), then the principle of divine priority is compromised. Ebeling therefore goes to great lengths to show that the Reformers were not seeking to replace one strand of tradition with another as the criterion of correct biblical interpretation. On the contrary, they wanted to replace the hermeneutical function of tradition with the claim that "the Holy Scriptures are the sole source of their own interpretation."[17] For Ebeling, the hermeneutical self-sufficiency of Scripture is necessary if the distinction between text and interpretation (and thus the logical priority of God over the church) is to be maintained.[18] While agreeing with Käsemann that the proper interpretation of Scripture is intimately connected with the free gift of grace, he also insists that this grace is neither reducible to nor capable of being guaranteed by any doctrinal formulation or interpretive tradition.[19]

Unfortunately, Ebeling's skill in identifying the theological issues at stake in the Scripture principle does not mean that he succeeds in addressing the difficulties to which Käsemann (whatever the shortcomings of his own proposal) points. From a Catholic perspective, Ebeling's refusal to concede a central hermeneutical role for the church and its traditions appears both naive and logically untenable, given the diversity of interpretations found in the history of Christian (not to mention non-Christian) reading of the Bible.[20] The substance of this objection can be summarized as follows: given that Protestant interpretation of Scripture has its own peculiar shape (one which is, moreover, often enshrined in their churches' written confessions of faith), on what basis do its practitioners claim to read Scripture independently of their own traditions?

Protestants may respond to this challenge by noting that they do not pretend to escape tradition; they just refuse to canonize it, thereby leaving themselves open to the witness of Scripture. Rhetorically effective as this retort may be, however, it is doubtful that it really gets to the heart of the Catholic objection, which centers precisely on the question of whether being genuinely open to Scripture as the Word of God (and not simply as a more or less interesting collection of human words) is possible apart from commitment to the established interpretive traditions of the church. Indeed, from a Catholic perspective, an insistence on Scripture alone is as likely as not to stifle Scripture's voice by a false abstraction of the meaning of the text from the situation of the interpreter.

AUTHORITY OF THE COMMUNITY AND RELIABILITY OF SCRIPTURE

This last point has been echoed strongly from within Protestant ranks by James Cone, who explicitly refuses to separate the authority of Jesus from the experience (or traditions) of black Christians.[21] Yet as strident as Cone may be in his insistence on the importance of the African American community in defining the parameters of faithful biblical interpretation, he takes great care to rule out the reduction of Scripture's meaning to the religious prejudices of the community of faith.[22]

Although the meaning of Scripture is correlated with black experience, it is not subordinated to it. Indeed, Cone contends that white Christians—especially the European American Protestant establishment—are the ones who stand guilty of allowing their cultural biases to distort their understanding of the Bible. Moreover, he argues that white failure to interpret Scripture rightly derives precisely from the quest for objective interpretation that regards the meaning of the text as independent of the situation of the interpreter.[23]

Modern European American debates over the relationship between faith and history serve as a case in point. Cone notes that while theologians on the right and the left have felt compelled to address the question of the Bible's historical accuracy, little attention has been paid to the impact of scriptural interpretation on the concrete shape of supposedly Christian societies.[24] In light of this situation, Cone suggests that the question of Scripture's meaning needs to be decoupled from the issue of its historicity. Not that Cone is inclined to minimize the importance of the Gospels' grounding in history. His point is simply that the meaning of Scripture cannot be secured in advance by historical-critical research; it is rather something that is established only in the course of its use by particular communities of faith.

Lest one suppose that Cone here gives in to a pragmatic understanding of scriptural authority, it is worth noting that Hans Frei (whose theological sensibilities are otherwise very different from Cone's) offers a similar critique of modern biblical hermeneutics. Frei argues that the Reformers were less interested in the historical truth of biblical narrative than in its ability to shape the church as a community of faith. Unlike contemporary liberals and fundamentalists alike, Luther and Calvin did not distinguish between the form and content of the biblical text in such a way as to suggest that Scripture's meaning and authority were dependent upon extraecclesial evaluations of its truth.[25] Instead, the meaning of the biblical texts, like that of a novel, was treated as a function of the interplay of character and circumstance found in the texts themselves:

> It is not going too far to say that the story is the meaning or, alternatively, that the meaning emerges from the story form, rather than being merely illustrated by it, as would be the case in allegory and in a different way, in myth. A great theme in literature of the novelistic type, like a pattern in historical sequence, cannot be paraphrased by a general statement. To do so would approach reducing it to meaninglessness. In each case the theme has meaning only to the extent that it is instantiated and hence narrated; and this meaning through instantiation is not *illustrated* . . . but

constituted through the mutual, specific determination of agents, speech, social context, and circumstances that form the indispensable narrative web.[26]

By contrast, Frei notes, fundamentalists and liberals alike tend to equate the meaning of the text with its historical reference, even if they disagree on the degree to which the biblical narrative corresponds to the historical facts.[27] According to Frei, this approach has produced a situation in which interpreters have lost sight of Scripture's narrative character: the text no longer constitutes its own universe of meaning but rather depends for its meaning on its successful ostensive reference to some feature (whether historical, ethical, or philosophical) of extratextual reality.[28] The paradoxical result of this process is that the biblical text has come to be viewed as much an obstacle as an aid to its own interpretation, since a proper reading requires penetrating behind the text in order to make contact with the reality to which it refers.

As described by Frei, the practice of critical exegesis introduced by the Enlightenment amounts to an implicit rejection of the Scripture principle. Instead of the biblical text providing the conceptual frame within which the world is interpreted, it is Scripture whose meaningfulness now depends on its compatibility with a wider frame of reference provided by historical research, philosophical anthropology, or some combination of the two.[29] While the Reformers certainly thought the biblical narratives were historically accurate, such considerations were secondary to (and derived from) the shape of the narratives themselves. Consequently, they experienced no tension between the meaning of the biblical texts and their historical referents, not primarily because they naively assumed the historical accuracy of the texts, but because the meaning of the texts was not understood as a function of their reference.

This ability to decouple the Bible's meaning from its historical reference, which Frei finds in the thought of the Reformers, is also characteristic of African American approaches to Scripture. It should therefore come as no surprise that the debates over biblical inerrancy that have plagued white Protestant theology for the past two centuries have not proved an issue in the black church.

According to Cone, this fact can be attributed to an implicit distinction in the black churches between Scripture's infallibility (or inerrancy) and its reliability.[30]

Reliability differs from infallibility in that it implies a communal context: a book is judged reliable because it has been experienced to be so in the life of the community. This is certainly not to suggest that the community thereby becomes the measure of Scripture's authority. On the contrary, the fact that Scripture has proved reliable implies precisely that the community has subordinated its own wisdom to that of the biblical texts. Indeed (as Cone suggests), the claim of biblical infallibility is far more likely to result in the community's imposition of its own preferences on a text that is regarded as fundamentally without mystery. Whereas the meaning of an infallible text all too easily may be viewed as given, the message contained in a reliable text must be worked out afresh in each new situation. That does not make the message contained in the text any less gracious, but it does mean recognizing that it is a grace that must be asked for, a treasure that must be sought, a door at which one must knock.

In trying to sort out the logical relationship between divine priority and the life of the community, the notion of the Bible as a reliable book functions as a good first approximation. It preserves scriptural priority while recognizing the role of the community in shaping a specifically Christian reading of the text. As opposed to theoretically ambitious concepts like inerrancy which are invoked as reasons why Scripture *should be* an object of interest, the idea of reliability simply points to the fact that Scripture *is* so regarded by Christians.

At this point, it might be objected that the Christian reading of Scripture, viewed disinterestedly, is just one possible hermeneutical option among many. But (for Frei and Cone alike) Christians do not claim to read the Bible disinterestedly; on the contrary, the Christian claim that the Bible is the Word of God means that it is to be read with a very special interest not associated with any other set of texts. Nor does this position constitute a surrender to relativism, as though the enthusiasm (or, for that matter, the simple existence) of a particular community were in itself an argument for the value of its hermeneutic. It is simply to recognize that a community's commitment to the priority of Scripture in the logic of Christian belief cannot be abstracted from the church's experience of the text's reliability.

ECCLESIOCENTRIC CHARACTER OF READING OF SCRIPTURE

The question remains, however, whether the community's role in regulating the use of Scripture does not finally evacuate the principle of *sola Scriptura* of its substance. The Reformers' insistence on *sola Scriptura* was born of the conviction that a fundamental rupture between the witness of the Bible and the life of the community was possible. And while the idea of scriptural reliability described by Cone certainly maintains a distinction between text and community (such that the community is definitely not free to interpret Scripture according to its own whim), it is not immediately clear how Scripture's priority with respect to the community of faith coheres with Cone's equal insistence that it is impossible to interpret Scripture correctly apart from solidarity with the oppressed.

The horns of the dilemma are clear. On one hand, if Scripture does not stand over against the church, then it will remain unclear whether the church truly speaks the Word of God, or simply proclaims the self-justification of human beings. On the other hand, sober reflection on the process of interpretation suggests that the idea of divine priority is itself a product of communal reflection and therefore inseparable from particular traditions of reading Scripture. In other words, if text needs to be distinguished from interpretation, it is also true that we have no access to the text except by way of particular interpretations.

The problem is complicated further by the fact that the principle of *sola Scriptura* implies nothing about the content of the biblical texts. The Scripture principle itself thus provides no criteria for evaluating any given instance of biblical interpretation; it has more the character of a grammatical rule specifying the place of Scripture in the logic of Christian belief. Its ablest defenders, beginning with Luther, have maintained that it is a necessary corollary of the Christian conviction regarding the logical priority of Christ. But just as Christ comes as the particular person Jesus, so Scripture comes only in the guise of particular interpretations, shaped by the ecclesial and cultural contexts of its readers.

To this extent, the idea that Scripture is hermeneutically self-sufficient seems something of an abstraction. Even Ebeling concedes that "since the truth of *sola Scriptura* depends on the reliable transmission of the Gospel, the Scripture-principle necessarily involves a doctrine of tradition."[31] And while he himself is fairly vague about the form such a doctrine would take, he does acknowledge that its necessity is grounded in the fact that the revelatory power of Scripture is inseparable from the life of the community, even if the latter is logically dependent on the former.[32]

Faced with the difficulty of reconciling these two apparently incompatible features of Christian reading of Scripture, New Testament scholar Richard Hays has attempted to correlate the church's reading of Scripture with God's own action of building the community, arguing that the Bible's own message of divine commitment to the community of faith demands that a genuinely Christian reading of Scripture be one in which the interpreter "makes the biblical text pass through the filter of God's action of forming the church."[33] If Hays is correct, then Scripture itself implies that the meaning of the text cannot be discussed in abstraction from the community it exists to instruct, so that a self-consciously ecclesiocentric reading of Scripture is justified on Scripture's own terms.

Hays himself is interested in trying to make sense of Pauline exegesis, not in developing a full-blown biblical hermeneutics; yet a way of reconciling the ecclesiocentric approach he describes with the principle of *sola Scriptura* is indirectly suggested by Hans Frei in the context of the Christological proposals in *The Identity of Jesus Christ*. As already noted, Frei contends that the influence of the Enlightenment has led theologians to try to justify Christian claims regarding Jesus' presence to believers in philosophical and historical terms instead of simply explicating the internal logic of that belief. That is, theologians have confused the assessment of the meaning of Christian claims with the quite different question of their truth as defined in historical-critical terms. Noting that none of these attempts has managed either to satisfy secular critics of Christianity or to produce consensus among the faithful, Frei, like Thiemann, proposes that theology bypass apologetic defenses of the faith in favor of a more modest effort to lay out the internal logic of Christian belief.[34]

Frei is interested in showing how Christian theological claims are rooted in hermeneutical conventions. But because he views his work as essentially descriptive rather than demonstrative, his conclusions regarding Christian beliefs about Jesus are no more than a restatement (albeit in much greater detail) of the basic assumption on which his inquiry is based.[35] This assumption is set forth clearly at the outset: "To have Christ present is to know who he is and to be persuaded that he lives. In our knowledge of Jesus Christ, his presence and identity are completely one. We cannot properly think of him as not present, as we can think of others without their real presence."[36]

It is open to question how widely this assumption would be accepted among communities that identify themselves as Christian. Also, notwithstanding Frei's eschewing of argument, it is hard to avoid reading his explication of the idea that Jesus' presence is implicit in his identity as an appeal for its truth. The point remains, however, that this appeal does not take the form of a logical demonstration through inference from a set of self-evident truths; it is rather a matter of showing that a proposition that certainly is subject to dispute (that Christ's identity implies his presence) is both internally coherent and consistent with a broad array of other Christian beliefs not in dispute.

In developing his thesis, Frei begins by noting that in all other cases knowledge of who a person is has no bearing on his or her presence to the knower, except in the trivial sense that in the act of knowing a person is present to the mind.[37] But, he argues, things are different with Jesus. In the same way that Anselm of Canterbury once argued that God is that being who cannot be conceived as not existing (since to understand who God is *eo ipso* to believe that God exists), so Frei holds that Jesus is the one who cannot be conceived as not present (since the claim that Christ is present is at the core of biblical description of who Jesus Christ is). Not that the two positions are identical. Anselm's argument is basically analytical: the assertion of God's existence is inferred from the definition of the word "God" as that than which nothing greater can be conceived. By contrast, Frei's argument is synthetic: that Christ is the one who is present does not derive immediately from the semantic value of the name "Jesus" or the title "Christ"; it is rather a function of way that the character Jesus of Nazareth is depicted in the canonical Gospels. Thus, it is not by virtue of a priori logical necessity but in light of the particular shape of the biblical narrative that Frei maintains:

> To grasp what this identity, Jesus of Nazareth . . . is, is to believe that he has been, *in fact,* raised from the dead. Someone may reply that in this case the most perfectly depicted character and most nearly lifelike fictional identity ought always in fact to have lived a factual historical life. We answer that the argument holds good only in this one and absolutely unique case, where the described entity . . . is totally identical with his factual existence. He *is* the resurrection and the life. How can he be conceived as not resurrected?[38]

While the immediate content of this argument is Christological, its force is hermeneutical: when Frei claims that understanding the identity of the biblical character Jesus of Nazareth entails recognition of his presence as risen Savior, he also implies that understanding Scripture means acknowledging its authority. For if recognition of Jesus' sovereignty is inseparable from the act of apprehending his identity, then understanding the texts that communicate this identity entails recognizing their authority as the medium of Jesus' own authoritative presence. As Frei puts it, the content of the biblical narrative is such that "complete commitment is [the] way of taking note of it."[39]

This line of argument provides a basis for filling out Luther's ideas about the clarity of Scripture. If the essential content of

Scripture is the story of Jesus Christ, and if this story is such that the identity of the Jesus it renders entails confession of that Jesus' presence, then it follows that Scripture is hermeneutically self-sufficient. If apprehension of Jesus' identity as given in Scripture entails recognition of Jesus' presence, then there is no reason to appeal to extrascriptural data in order to identify the object of Christian faith.[40] And yet this position does not involve any claim that the canonical texts possess supernatural qualities (such as might be associated with a theory of biblical inspiration, for example) that render their meaning and authority uniquely transparent. Quite the contrary, Frei's argument is based on a theoretically low-level hermeneutic according to which one approaches Scripture in much the same way as one would a novel. What sets the Gospels apart is simply that the identity they cumulatively render is one in which identity and presence are given together.

Nor, from this perspective, does the fact of disagreement among Christians regarding the meaning of particular texts render the Scripture principle untenable. Frei does not claim that the meaning of every biblical text is self-evident, but only that there is no firmer logical ground outside Scripture on the basis of which exegetical disagreements might be resolved. Because Jesus is uniquely and unsubstitutably identified in the Gospels as the one who is present, the attempt to find a hermeneutical criterion outside of Scripture against which the Gospel rendering of his identity might be assessed (as one might do when reading a conventional biography, for example) indicates only that the reader has failed to grasp the identity of Jesus in the first place. After all, the search for such a criterion presupposes that the identity rendered in the narrative is only incompletely accessible to the reader—and thus only makes sense on the assumption that the character rendered is *not* present. But because Jesus is present in the Gospel accounts, the Christian who wishes to plumb the depths of Jesus' identity is always driven by the logic of that identity back to the biblical text. And while Frei concedes that one does not have to read Scripture as a Christian, he maintains that even the reader who objects to the claims Christians make about Jesus can certainly understand the hermeneutical logic according to which those claims are made; namely, that in this one case, to understand the meaning of the texts involves the recognition that they claim a uniquely authoritative status for their own interpretation.[41]

As persuasive as Frei's reasoning may be, however, it may legitimately be asked to what extent texts, biblical or otherwise, can "claim" something. This bit of anthropomorphism might be permitted if it were the case that texts could be read in only one way, but Frei's own critique of post-Enlightenment hermeneutics rests on the observation that the biblical texts can, in fact, be read in a number of ways, some of which are not at all consistent with his own approach. It should therefore come as no surprise that in his later work Frei himself concedes that his own preference for a narrative reading of Scripture already presupposes a specifically Christian orientation to the biblical text.[42] In this way, he recognizes that particular communities, and not the texts considered in themselves, are properly the subject of claims about how Scripture is to be read.[43] Yet he nowhere confronts the theological implications of recognizing the community's role in determining what counts as a specifically Christian reading of the biblical texts, notwithstanding the fact that to concede such a constitutive hermeneutical role to the community would appear to undermine the priority of Scripture.

To avoid this result without compromising the substance of Frei's insights regarding the interrelationship between the priority of Jesus and the structure of the biblical narrative, it is necessary to make a case that the narrative itself somehow implicates the community in the rendering of Jesus' identity. In this way, appeal to the interpretive practice of the community of faith would not mean introducing an extrascriptural factor into the hermeneutical process but would rather follow from Scripture itself.

While Frei himself does not take this step, he does point this way to the kind of correlation between the life of the community and Jesus' identity when he makes the following observation regarding the relationship between the identity of Jesus and that of the covenant community of Israel: "At the end of the story, as at its beginning, there is full identity between Jesus and Israel. But whereas at the beginning it was the community that served to identify him, the reverse is now the case. He, Jesus, provides the community . . . with his identity. He is the Christ of Israel who, in his own singular identity and unsubstitutable history, sums up and identifies the history of the whole people."[44]

Frei here points to the pivotal role of Jesus in the narrative trajectory of the Gospel accounts, but the schema he presents has obvious implications for the Christian reading of the canon as a whole. Because the Gospel narratives that render the identity of Jesus presuppose the story of Israel narrated in the Hebrew Scriptures, the Old Testament books are just as crucial (and thus unsubstitutable) for the rendering of Jesus' identity as are the Gospels. Insofar as the history of Israel is brought to a climax in the evangelists' depiction of Jesus, it follows that the rendering of Jesus' identity is inseparable from the rendering of the identity of the community of Israel. As Frei also notes, however, the history of the community does not simply come to an end with Jesus; on the contrary, even as Jesus sums up the history of the community, he also gives the community an expanded mission as the church.[45] Because this redefinition of the covenant community is inseparable from the rendering of Jesus' identity, being in that community is not a logically distinct consequence of knowing Jesus (as though one first knew Jesus and then recognized that this implied life in community). Rather, in the same way that knowledge of Jesus is inseparable from commitment to him, it is also inseparable from participation in the life of the community he identifies. Jesus' presence, as entailed by his narratively rendered identity, is realized in and to the community of believers.[46]

Therefore, although Frei's narrative approach to Scripture means that any attempt to further one's understanding of who Jesus is necessarily leads one back to the biblical texts, Christians find that the scriptural narrative itself implicates the community in the rendering of Jesus' identity in such a way that to be referred to Scripture is at the same time to be referred to the community. It can therefore remain a firm principle of Christian reading of Scripture that Jesus' identity is uniquely and unsubstitutably rendered by the narrative, at the same time that it is also recognized that the biblical depiction of Jesus so involves the community of those who confess him that the substance of his identity (which is, after all, nothing other than Jesus' continuing presence in the community) cannot be grasped apart from the community. In other words, because the Gospel narratives depict a Jesus who has identified his destiny fully with that of the church, Jesus' identity—and thus his authority—is inseparable from the church's life.

CONCLUSIONS

I have attempted to defend the coherence of the Scripture principle while acknowledging the ecclesial mediation of biblical interpretation by arguing that the church can plausibly view itself as implicated in Scripture's rendering of Jesus' identity and authority. My argument may be schematized as follows:

1. Knowledge of Jesus' identity is sufficiently and unsubstitutably rendered in the Gospel narratives.
2. The sufficiency of the biblical rendering of Jesus' identity derives from the fact that Jesus is identified as the one who is present.
3. But Jesus' scripturally rendered identity is also inseparable from the identity of the believing community with which he both is identified and identifies himself.
4. Therefore, Jesus' identity is inseparable from reference to the community with which he identifies.

This chain of reasoning brings the argument full circle: it begins from the assumption that the meaning of Scripture is *the identity of Jesus,* while its conclusion implies that the meaning of Scripture (precisely insofar as it successfully renders Jesus' identity) is inseparable from the *identity of the community.* This circularity suggests that there is nothing inconsistent about invoking the Scripture principle within a self-consciously communal matrix of biblical interpretation, since the community's claim to authority (as exercised in its interpretation of Scripture) is inseparable from its commitment to Jesus' authority (and thus to the priority of Scripture).

This is not to say that this way of understanding the church's relationship to Scripture is the only plausible one, for the church has no reason to deny the possibility of internally coherent readings of Scripture other than its own. Indeed, to characterize the church's experience of Scripture as reliable is implicitly to recognize that the church's way of reading Scripture is specific to the church. But the recognition that there is no universal, objective justification for the way of reading Scripture I propose does not mean it is simply arbitrary. If my proposal cannot be defended in absolute terms, it can be justified on the (relative) grounds that it is the best way of incorporating a broad array of other Christian beliefs about Scripture and the faith community.

By making a case that Scripture itself, in the course of depicting the identity of Jesus of Nazareth, ascribes to the community a crucial role in rendering the biblical subject matter, the model I propose preserves the logical priority of Scripture. For while it is true that Scripture renders Jesus' identity only within the conceptual frame constituted by the faith community, the action of the community (along with its attendant conceptual frames) is a feature authorized by that same narrative. The resulting picture is one in which (to cite Richard Hays once more) "Scripture continues to speak in order to call into existence the community in which it can be heard rightly."[47]

The claim that a self-consciously ecclesiocentric hermeneutic is not necessarily inconsistent with *sola Scriptura* certainly does not amount to a general apologetic strategy for the Christian faith, nor should it even be regarded as a means toward the construction of such an apologetics. Its aim is rather the more limited one of showing that the circularity involved in explaining the relationship between the biblical text and the ecclesial matrix within which it is interpreted need not be vicious. This claim, if substantiated, provides a starting point for addressing the broader problem of the relationship between divine priority and human activity.

By itself, however, assigning the community a constitutive role in scriptural interpretation does not constitute an adequate response to the contemporary challenges to the church's authority noted in the introduction. For one thing, it does not explain how the dependence of the community's authority on that of Jesus is to be distinguished from the community claiming authority on its own account. While one may be able to argue on a formal level that the community is subject to the authority of the text (and even concede that in the particular case of the American slaves a theological commitment to the collective experience of the community happened to be combined with an equally fervent dedication to the biblical witness), materially this kind of ecclesiocentrism seems to offer no impediment to a de facto undermining of scriptural autonomy in which God's action can no longer be distinguished from that of the church.

THE POLITICS OF THEOLOGY AND THE CHURCH'S IDENTITY

The aim of the argument thus far has been to take the first steps in developing a coherent alternative to theological strategies that center on a doctrine of revelation. Revelational theologies founder because they fail to do equal justice to Christian belief in the priority of God as the ultimate source of theological claims and the integrity of human beings as agents capable of responding to them. This failure can be described still more precisely: theologies that take the doctrine of revelation as their point of departure do not recognize the unavoidable circularity of the relationship between the ecclesiocentric and Christocentric dimensions of theological reflection.

In the otherwise laudable desire to preserve the priority of divine over human action, proponents of the doctrine of revelation typically refuse to allow the church a constitutive role in shaping the terms of Christian faith and practice. By isolating Scripture as an objective manifestation of divine will, Protestant theologians in particular do not take sufficient account of the biblical interpreter's participation in (and implicit commitment to) the hermeneutical conventions of her or his community of faith.

The circular relationship between the ecclesiocentric and Christocentric dimensions of Christian theology in general and of biblical interpretation in particular is not necessarily vicious. The church's role in regulating hermeneutical practice can be derived from the content of Scripture itself, insofar as the biblical narrative links God's identity and presence specifically to the life of the covenant community. Because God is depicted in Scripture as one who wills to live in communion with humankind, and because this will is realized in the ministry of Jesus of Nazareth, the presence (and thus the authority) of God is inseparable from the church as that community with whose story God's own is irrevocably linked.

By affirming in this way the inseparability of divine and ecclesial authority without equating the two, it is possible to account for the role of the community in regulating Christian practice without compromising the theological priority of God which the principle of *sola Scriptura* is designed to preserve. The argument can be summarized as follows: the church's exercise of authority in defining and regulating a distinctively Christian way of reading Scripture falls within the larger context of divine priority so long as the church's role in interpreting Scripture can be shown to be dependent upon the witness of Scripture itself. That is, although the church exercises authority when it defines and enforces a distinctively Christian way of reading Scripture, it does so with the understanding that even this authority is dependent on the church's having first subjected itself to Scripture's authority.

PROBLEMS WITH AN ECCLESIOCENTRIC VIEW OF CHURCH AUTHORITY

It is one thing to make a formal distinction between ecclesial and divine authority and quite another to specify the practical implications of this distinction for the church's life. Although the church's authority may remain subject to the test of Scripture in theory, it is not immediately clear how Scripture's priority is to be enforced in practice, given the church's role in shaping Christian interpretation of Scripture. On logical as well as political grounds, the church would seem all too easily tempted to view any theological challenge to its established practice as the product of an alternative way of reading Scripture that, by definition, places the would-be critic outside the community of faith. Yet once this de facto immunity from criticism is granted, the formal distinction between the original authority of God and the derived authority of the church is evacuated of material significance for the life of the community.

Even such an extreme position could not easily be dismissed as incoherent. The theological problems associated with the merging of ecclesial and divine identity do not result from logical difficulties, but from the fact that such a merger cannot be squared with what seems to be clear scriptural witness that the covenant community is subject to error and, therefore, periodically in need of theological correction (see, for example, 1 Cor. 4:8–13; 2 Cor. 13:5–10; Gal. 1:6–7; Rev. 2:1–3:22).

Such criticism is obviously impossible if the authority of the community is identified with that of God in a way that requires any criticism of ecclesial practice to be interpreted as blasphemy. Thus, while there is no a priori reason why divine priority over the community could not be limited to the purely formal sphere, such a position is unconvincing because it is inconsistent with the biblical picture of the covenant community. In this context, it is an important corollary of the Scripture principle that God's priority with respect to the church is realized when individual Christians critique existing practice on the basis of Scripture. If criticism of the community is ruled out in practice, then neither God nor the individual believer retains any independent theological significance over against the community, under which both are effectively subsumed.

To be sure, even the Reformers recognized that it was necessary to treat some deviations from established church practice as tantamount to a forfeiture of church membership. Nor is this surprising: if Christian practice is bound up with a particular way of reading Scripture, advocates of alternative practices (even if they base their arguments on Scripture) are open to the charge of having failed to read Scripture in this particular way. Unless the church is willing to forfeit its existence as a distinct community with a distinct message, the possibility of making this kind of judgment must be allowed. But it must also be recognized that the logic of Christian belief does not demand such a verdict in response to *every* critique of the status quo. Consequently, it is necessary to ask what criteria are to be used to distinguish those critiques which rightly demand the church's attention from those which do not.

This question cannot be answered without taking into account the reality of political inequality within the church. While, formally speaking, any intraecclesial dispute can be viewed as a matter of two individuals (or groups of individuals) loyal to the same tradition disagreeing over its implications for a particular practice, the ecclesiastical status of the individuals involved may be expected to be of immense practical significance in the final outcome This is not to deny that there may be good theological as well as practical reasons for such disparity between members of the community of faith. Once it is conceded that the church can, in principle, speak with authority, there is no basis for regarding the exercise of that authority by an established body of leaders as inherently suspect.

Scripture itself provides ample support for the view that the authority of the community's leaders is more than a matter of sociological accident (see, for example, Matt. 16:18–19; John 20:22–23; 1 Tim. 4:11–14); indeed, several passages go so far as to suggest that the authority of the office is to be respected even when those who exercise it are open to reproach (Matt. 23:2–3; compare Acts 23:3–5).[1]

As the agents through whom the stories and practices that define the community are preserved, the church's official leadership can be viewed as the precipitate of God's work of building up the community over time, and thus as a phenomenon with genuine theological significance.[2] Because the church risks being blown about by every new wind of doctrine where the sociological anchor of a well-defined center is lacking, the existence of an imbalance of power between those individuals close to the communal center and those who are not can be viewed as the consequence of God's own commitment to preserve the church as a distinct community over time.

Having conceded this much, however, it is immediately necessary to add that the legitimate authority of those at the communal center does not preclude their being subject to critique by other segments of the community. That Christians over the centuries have rejected established groups ranging from Gnostics to German Christians shows that ecclesiastical authority has not been conceded to everyone who has exercised it. Moreover, because these acts of rejection involve the critique of particular practices, it follows that critique of established leaders, far from automatically constituting a threat to communal identity, may at least sometimes prove necessary for its preservation.

Recognizing that the leadership is in no way immune from grave theological error, Dietrich Bonhoeffer, for example, couples words of appreciation for the value of an established church (as identified by the official leadership) with a frank acknowledgment of the dangers that go with its inherent conservatism. In this context, he even envisions the possibility that in certain circumstances, it might prove theologically necessary for the church to disestablish itself.[3] So long as Christians recognize the possibility that a valid critique of the ecclesiastical establishment may be mounted by individuals removed from power, it is necessary to concede that at any given time, the political center of the community may not coincide with the theological center defined by God's activity of building the community through the gospel.[4] The challenge of the present chapter is to defend this possibility without diluting the force of God's identification with the church in Jesus Christ.

Critique of a particular practice does not by itself constitute a judgment against the ecclesial identity of the community as a whole, any more than the fact that a community acknowledges the possibility of excommunication necessarily indicates a zero tolerance for theological debate. Christianity is rarely conceived as a system of practices for which complete agreement is a condition of participation, as shown by the fact that even churches that stress the importance of agreement in matters of faith often tolerate a significant degree of theological diversity in practice. In any case, the biblical injunctions to test all aspects of communal faith and practice (1 Thess. 5:21; 2 Cor. 13:5; Gal. 6:4; Eph. 5:10; 1 John 4:1) suggest the need for ongoing debate over correct practice in the church. These considerations notwithstanding, it is necessary to focus on those cases where the community, as identified by its leadership, *does* cease to be the church (a possibility that the biblical witness also affirms; see, for example, Matt. 18:15–17; 1 Cor. 16:22; Gal. 1:8–9; Rev. 2:6), because it is where they are concerned that the critique of church practice seems most difficult to reconcile with the ecclesiocentric aspects of theology.

Once again, the terms of the dilemma are easily stated. If the community's identity as church can be questioned on theological grounds, how can participation in that same community be regarded as a necessary point of reference for theological reflection? Likewise, if Scripture can be used to show that the community is not the church, how is it possible to claim that the community functions as the necessary context for the correct reading of Scripture? And yet a community immune from such condemnation would be so closely identified with God as to evacuate the confession of divine priority of any practical significance. If this latter result is to be avoided, it is necessary to give some attention to the question the Reformers addressed under the rubric of the "marks of the church."

MARKS OF THE CHURCH AS CONSTRAINTS ON READING SCRIPTURE

Because the problem of distinguishing the true church from the false presupposes the possibility of radical discontinuity between ecclesial practice and divine will, it is in many respects complementary to the analysis of *sola Scriptura* presented in chapter 3. Like the Scripture principle, the identification of the marks of the church (*notae ecclesiae*) was first addressed systematically during the Reformation period. Nor should this historical point be passed over too quickly, for, unlike earlier schisms between Chalcedonians and Monophysites or Rome and Constantinople, the Reformation's shattering of western European "Christendom" forced the Reformers to view the task of distinguishing the true church from the false as a concretely sociological problem no less than a theological one.[5]

Luther, for example, believed that what he took to be the creed's identification of the "holy, catholic church" with the "communion of saints" was an adequate theological definition of the church but deficient in that it left open the question of how this assembly was to be recognized in the world.[6] In the same context, Calvin distinguished the invisible church, the reality of which was a matter of faith, from the imperfect, visible communities with which Christians were confronted.[7]

Insofar as both Reformers continued to define the church in terms of the categories of the ecumenical creeds, their conflict with Rome was not primarily over how the church was to be understood doctrinally, but over where it was to be found in the world. Previously, when ecclesiastical unity had been a matter of sociological fact, this issue was not especially pressing; but as soon as some Christian churches refused to concede that status to other claimants within the same cultural and political sphere (in this case, that of western Europe), the question of the criteria by which the church could be identified became of a matter of central importance.

These sociological dimensions of the issue notwithstanding, however, the Reformers connected the need to specify marks of the church with the fact that the church, as "an association of faith and of the Holy Spirit in [human] hearts," could not simply be equated with the sociological reality of the "outward ties and rites" confronting human beings in history.[8] Thus, while the Reformers regarded ecclesiology as inseparable from sociology, they did not believe it could be reduced to institutional structures.

Indeed, they insisted that the earthly church, made up of fallible human beings living under the constraints of time and space, was necessarily a very imperfect manifestation of the holy and catholic church triumphant. On this point, Catholics agreed; indeed, a good part of the ensuing debate resulted from the fact that Catholic theologians did not see how the Reformers could agree with them in affirming that a community's ecclesial status did not depend on the sanctity of its membership,[9] and yet continue to frame their critique of Rome in terms of the institutional church's imperfections.[10]

At this point, the ecclesiological positions correspond to their attitudes with respect to the Scripture principle. For Catholics, everything hinged on the inseparability of Christian faith and practice from the structures and policies of the institutional church: because a practice can only be recognized as Christian in the first place insofar as it is integrated into the life of the established Christian community, to invoke allegedly Christian criteria over against this community's practice involved a contradiction. The Reformers' claim to be able to judge the ecclesial status of the Roman church appeared to constitute an implicit denial of the necessary imperfection of the church militant, since only on the assumption that such imperfection had been overcome did it seem possible to acquire a position over against the community from which to judge it.

The Reformers refused to accept this construal of their position. Though the Scripture principle was not always explicitly invoked by the Reformers in ecclesiological controversies, it is clearly reflected in their insistence that it was possible to make an effective distinction between divine and human will only by affirming that the church's established authorities could be in error. To Protestant eyes, it was the Catholics who were in danger of obliterating the distinction between the church militant and the church triumphant.[11] By introducing the concept of "marks of the church," the Reformers sought to reaffirm this distinction without compromising the reality of the church as concrete, historical community:

> We are not dreaming about some Platonic republic, as has been slanderously alleged, but we teach that this church actually exists, made up of true believers and righteous men scattered throughout the world. And we add its marks, the pure teaching of the Gospel and the [right administration of] the sacraments. . . . Of course, there are also many weak people in it who build on this foundation perishing structures of stubble, that is, unprofitable opinions. But because they do not overthrow the foundation, these are forgiven them or even corrected.[12]

Admittedly, someone needs to decide exactly what constitutes "pure teaching of the Gospels . . . and the sacraments." Once that decision has been made, however, it would seem to be a comparatively easy matter to discover which communities subscribe to the standard thus defined: one need do no more than ask them.

Nor was the task of specifying the "pure teaching of the Gospel" logically problematic for the Reformers, given their commitment to the principle of scriptural clarity. As previously noted, this principle was the cornerstone of the Reformers' insistence on the logical priority of Scripture over the community of faith. Because the gospel is the good news that our salvation is accomplished entirely by Jesus, and because Jesus is encountered uniquely and unsubstitutably in Scripture, it is impossible to deny Scripture's clarity without rendering our encounter with Jesus (and thus our participation in the salvation he brings) uncertain.[13] And while the Reformers had no interest in trying to separate the exposition of Scripture from the life of the church,[14] they insisted that Scripture grounds the community, and not vice versa.[15] Consequently, when it came to defining the criteria for determining "pure teaching of the Gospel," they maintained that Scripture was "the only true norm according to which all teachers and teachings are to be judged and evaluated."[16]

This point made, it remained only to specify, in suitably concise form, what the "pure teaching of the Gospel" was. To this end, both Lutherans and Calvinists resorted to written confessions as summaries of "pure teaching" which could be used to evaluate a community's claims to be the church. Insofar as these confessions were understood as practical expedients composed in the context of particular doctrinal debates ("to refute heresies, and to give public confession of the faith to the generations following"),[17] however, they were themselves subject to the test of Scripture. And though they served as summary descriptions of the way in which the community read Scripture, confessions were not understood as mere expressions of communal opinion.[18]

Despite the fact that they were composed with the explicit intent of clarifying the doctrinal position of particular churches, however, confessions often provoked as many theological questions as they resolved. Most obviously, confessions were themselves subject to different interpretations and thus needed to be supplemented by new confessions as fresh controversies arose.[19] While the periodic writing of new confessions was always possible (and continues to be standard practice in the Reformed tradition), the fact that written confessions are subject to differing interpretations indicates that formal adherence to them is not in itself sufficient to identify the true church. Even if it is agreed that any modifications to a confession must be tested at the bar of Scripture, it is not clear how that criterion is to be applied when the meaning of the community's confessional blueprint for reading Scripture is itself the subject of controversy.

Nor is the potential for ambiguity the only problem with written confessions. Notwithstanding their agreement that confessional formulations needed to be tested against the witness of Scripture, their tendency to regard confessional orthodoxy as both a necessary *and* a sufficient mark of the church led Lutherans and Calvinists alike to try to eliminate any grounds for debate over church practice through more precise and exhaustive confessional language. Whatever the benefits of this approach for ensuring ecclesiastical stability, it ultimately fails to come to terms with the community's role in defining the parameters of Christian reading of Scripture.

To regard a written confession as not only necessary but also sufficient to resolve all doctrinal disputes certainly does not avoid the problem of attributing undue authority to the community in scriptural interpretation. At best, it simply pushes the question of the role of the community in defining and applying confessional norms back a step. At worst, it leads to a situation in which doctrines cease to function as a convenient summary of Scripture's meaning and instead supersede Scripture as the norm for the community's talk about God. Since the adoption of a communally formulated and interpreted confession is by itself insufficient to protect the church against this temptation, it appears that further marks of the church need to be identified.

Although neither the Lutheran nor the Calvinist branch of the Reformation was quick to recognize the logical difficulties attending dependence on written confessions, both movements did recognize other marks of the church. As already noted, the Lutheran confessional documents coupled the pure teaching of the gospel with the proper administration of the sacraments,[20] and Calvin agreed that these two marks were an infallible sign of the church's presence.[21]

Yet the number of marks was not always limited to two. The Scots Confession added "ecclesiastical discipline uprightly ministered,"[22] while Luther himself enumerated no less than seven "marks" in his treatise "On the Councils and the Church."[23] And while this large number results from the fact that Luther counted separately the rites that might in another context be included under the generic term "sacraments" (for example, baptism, eucharist, absolution, ordained ministry, and public worship), we are still left with the rather surprising mark of public persecution alongside the usual criterion of pure preaching.[24] In any case, Luther's essay shows that the number of marks of the church may vary considerably even within a fairly narrowly defined confessional tradition. Is there a basic level of consensus to be discerned in the various lists?

I would like to suggest that there is such a basic level of agreement and, more specifically, that it parallels the liberationist concern for the character of communal action (orthopraxy) in addition to the content of doctrine (orthodoxy). This is not in any way to minimize the considerable theological and ecclesiological differences between various Protestant positions; nor is it to argue that the much more detailed insights of contemporary liberation theology find anything but the vaguest anticipation in Reformation thought. It is only to suggest that both Lutheran and Reformed shared an understanding of the "marks of the church" in which evaluation of what Christians believe cannot be separated from the question of how they believe it.

That some such consolidation in the list of the church's marks is warranted is rendered at least initially plausible by the otherwise rather trivial point that neither Luther nor his followers seem to have felt much discomfort over the disparity between the number of marks in "On the Councils and the Church" and the Augsburg Confession. Here, as elsewhere, numbers were not regarded as being of central importance.[25]

One dare not be so blithe in evaluating the differences between Lutheran and Reformed emphasis on the significance of ecclesiastical order, but here, too, the difference may not be as great as first appears. Clearly, there is a real disagreement: the Reformed tradition stresses that a particular form of ecclesial polity is mandated by Scripture, and Lutherans do not. Nor should the practical significance of this dispute for the subsequent history of the two communions (or for the overall shape of their respective theologies) be underestimated.

All the same, it remains the case that neither tradition regards church order as a matter of sheer indifference. The Lutheran confessions repeatedly recognize the need for an established church order and insist that the form such an order takes is subject to certain constraints.[26] The disagreement between the two traditions is more a matter of how strictly those constraints are drawn;[27] for neither one is any order whatsoever acceptable. Given that the Scots Confession itself includes issues of order in its discussion of proper administration of the sacraments (not to mention Calvin's own agreement in the *Institutes* with the confessional Lutheran numbering of marks),[28] it seems legitimate, for the purposes of the present argument, to conclude that both branches of the Reformation share the conviction that a community claiming to be the church has to be evaluated both according to the orthodoxy of its confession and the orthopraxy of its communal life, however the content of either category may be spelled out in detail.

Admittedly, the Reformers themselves were not always particularly clear in specifying exactly how these two criteria might be combined in practice to provide a functional program of internal dogmatic critique. Thus, while the written confessions produced in the Reformed churches all presupposed the priority of Scripture, neither Lutherans nor Calvinists spent much energy exploring how the ways in which a confession is drawn from (and, subsequently, applied to) the Bible might be as important as its verbal content in preserving the functional (as opposed to the merely theoretical) priority of Scripture.

Consequently, among both groups a community's ecclesial status was invariably determined by reference to its confessional orthodoxy rather than its practice. As already noted, the major weakness of this emphasis on written confessions as the principal line of defense against ecclesial subjectivity is that confessions are themselves no more than the precipitate of communal consensus. And yet a defining feature of the Scripture principle to which both these branches of the Reformation subscribed was the principle that communal consensus is not an adequate criterion of theological truth. In order to be theologically binding, such consensus must be congruent with the witness of Scripture.

As argued in chapter 3, scriptural priority is bound up with a particular set of hermeneutical conventions according to which Scripture is read as a unified narrative centered in the story of Jesus. Combined with the analysis of written confessions presented in this chapter, the conclusion follows that these *procedural* norms for biblical interpretation cannot be measured solely by reference to *doctrinal* criteria. Further attention to the total context of ecclesial practice is required.

Therefore, while appeal to a written confession as the framework for a community's understanding of Scripture certainly does impose certain constraints on hermeneutical practice, it leaves open the question of how a community arrives at and regulates its confessional stance. Specifically, a confessional theology in the style of the Reformation fails to reckon sufficiently with the possibility that a written confession may come to supersede Scripture as the defining norm of Christian practice. If this danger is to be avoided, it is necessary to look behind the day-to-day experience of communal consensus to examine the specific processes by which a community's confessional stance is shaped.

Specifically, it is important to keep in mind that "marks of the church" can be used to distinguish the true church from the false only where the individual Christian is able to serve as the means through which Scripture exercises its normative function over the church. Because every specific act of biblical interpretation has its roots in the activity of an individual, the exercise of individual responsibility in the reading of Scripture is a necessary condition of the community's having any distinctive teaching at all.

Yet while it is true that all concrete acts of interpretation are the work of individuals, the fact that not all individuals enjoy the same status with respect to the community's own internal structures of authority all too easily leads to a situation in which only those individuals who enjoy positions of authority within the community are able to shape communal practice, while voices on the periphery are either ignored or suppressed. This state of affairs would appear to suppress the possibility of criticizing the status quo that the Reformers wished to preserve—unless we can find theological reasons for counteracting the community's natural inertia by giving peripheral voices greater weight.

chapter five

CHRISTIAN CONFESSION AND THE IDENTITY OF JESUS CHRIST

Despite the shortcomings of Reformation theologies, there is still good reason to interpret Jesus' priority over the traditions of the faith community in terms of the category of confession. Whether in the context of repentance (the generally private confession of sins before Christ) or proclamation (the generally public confession of faith in Christ), the term "confession" has long been used in the church to express personal commitment to Jesus Christ.

CONFESSION AS A BASIS FOR CRITICISM OF COMMUNAL PRACTICE

This combination of public and private connotations reflects the idea that commitment to Jesus entails both assuming a position over against others and recognizing a measure of responsibility to them. As the Reformers understood, the act of confession provides an objective basis for a community's identity as church and, thereby, a means by which an individual can affirm his or her own relationship to Jesus. Where the churches of the Reformation fell short was in their increasingly static understanding of confession as a definitive doctrinal summary, which (in principle if not in practice) could be fixed in writing for all time.

By contrast, the biblical understanding of confession is far more dynamic. The Greek verb *homologein* (an exact parallel to the Latin *confiteri,* from which the English word "confession" is derived) means literally "to speak together with" someone else. And while the word can mean simply "to agree," its use in the New Testament generally encompasses far more than shared opinion. For example, when Jesus declares, "Whoever shall confess me before others, I shall confess before [God] in heaven" (Matt. 10:32), he requires an act of public solidarity that has as much to do with the conditions under which one speaks (practice) as with what one says (doctrine).[1]

As expressed in Matthew 10:32, the rationale for this demand seems fairly simple: if you want Jesus to stand with you on Judgment Day, you need to stand with him now. And Jesus leaves little doubt that standing with him is to be taken quite literally. The disciples are commended because they leave everything to follow Jesus (Matt. 19:27–29 and pars.). By contrast, Jesus is critical of those who speak well of him but hesitate when it comes to sharing the conditions of his physical existence (see Matt. 8:18–22 and par.; 19:21–23 and pars.; compare 7:21–23; 21:28–32).

That is not to say that confession of Jesus Christ involves obliterating one's own identity. The point of Matthew 10:32 is just the opposite: the fact that in faith we find ourselves unable to say who we are apart from Jesus anticipates the fact that on the last day Jesus will be unable to give a final account of himself to God apart from us. The confession of which Jesus speaks is an act of solidarity in which the individual defines her or his own identity in terms of relationship with Jesus, who has already staked *his* identity as the Christ on the will to live—and die—in relationship with us.

It is an open question entirely whether or not we should wish to live in relationship with Jesus of Nazareth. But the point remains that confession of Jesus is more than a matter of words. It is not sufficient for the Christian to say the right things about Jesus while keeping a safe distance from him. In this way, *con*fession needs to be distinguished from mere *pro*fession, in which all that is required is assent to a particular sequence of words. Defined as the act of speaking together with another, the content of a confession is inseparable from the circumstances under which it is made. It is therefore not possible to confess Jesus without taking seriously the question of where Jesus is to be found.

The fact that Jesus has first drawn near to us remains the presupposition of the confessional act of drawing near to Jesus. Finding Jesus, therefore, can never be interpreted as a matter of human merit. Yet it is also true that Jesus comes to establish a relationship between God and humankind that calls for our active participation—and thereby includes the possibility of our refusal. That we may act on this possibility in no way mitigates Jesus' commitment to our lives; it merely signifies that we have opted out of his.[2]

A more serious problem is how we can find Jesus in the world, given the Christian conviction that in the resurrection Jesus has definitively transcended the limitations of space and time (see 2 Cor. 5:16; compare John 17:11). This issue can only be addressed in a satisfactory manner when due emphasis is placed on the claim that the one raised from the dead is none other than Jesus. Notwithstanding the diversity of their perspectives on the resurrection, the New Testament writers all begin from the position that it is impossible to divorce the identity and presence of the one who was raised on Easter morning from the particularity of the man from Nazareth who was crucified on Good Friday afternoon. So while it is true that Jesus is no longer among us "according to the flesh," it is also true that who Jesus is in heaven is inseparable from who he was in time and space. Specifically, if Jesus ends his earthly life on the cross, and if this ending is constitutive of his identity as the one who was raised, then for us who continue on earth, confessing Jesus is inseparable from following the path he took to Calvary.

That Jesus himself instructed his followers to take up their cross and follow him does not make it any easier to discern this path. Apart from the fact that our own lives are far removed from first-century Palestine, the situation is complicated by the fact that Jesus' ministry stretched from Galilee to Jerusalem, from the Temple courts to the Gentile towns of the Decapolis, and from the tombs of Gadara to Pharisees' homes. These widely different settings have little in common other than their status as settings for Jesus' proclaiming that God's realm is near (see, for example, Matt. 4:17, 23; 5:3,10; 8:11; 10:7; 12:28; 19:23–24; 21:31, 43; 23:13; 24:14 and pars.). Yet if the breadth of this mission seems initially to obscure its contours, things come into focus as soon as it is recognized that it is precisely the all-embracing character of the realm he proclaims that brings Jesus into conflict with established powers. The shape of this conflict serves as a measure of Jesus' own model status as the one "who bore witness before Pontius Pilate by making the good confession" (1 Tim. 6:12–13).

That Jesus' status as confessor is linked to his trial highlights the degree to which the confession he models is not reducible to a matter of words. For while it is impossible to know exactly which account of Jesus' trial the writer of 1 Timothy had in mind, the most striking characteristic of the Gospel accounts of the trial before Pilate is precisely Jesus' silence: "Now Jesus stood before the governor; and the governor questioned him, saying, 'Are you the king of the Jews?' Jesus said, 'You say so.' And when he was accused by the high priests and the elders, he made no answer at all. Then Pilate said to him, 'Don't you hear all the charges they make against you?' But Jesus did not answer him a single word, so that the governor was greatly amazed" (Matt. 27:11–14; compare Mark 15:2–5; Luke 23:2–5).[3]

The "confession" described in these lines impresses Pilate, but it certainly does not qualify as a definitive summary of Christian belief. It does, however, suggest that Jesus' words (or lack thereof) cannot be assessed apart from the setting in which they are spoken. Once it is recognized that where and how Jesus speaks is every bit as important as (because constitutive of) what he says, it becomes easier to understand how his preaching of God's realm, though received by some as gospel, could be viewed by Pilate and others as a threat.

Although we have taken the trial before Pilate as our point of departure, it is important to remember that conflict is not a late or isolated development in Jesus' career. On the contrary, the Gospels describe a persistent pattern according to which Jesus' preaching arouses suspicion or even outright hostility among various groups. In Luke's Gospel, this tension goes all the way back to the beginning of Jesus' public ministry in an episode worth quoting in its entirety:

And he came to Nazareth, where he had grown up, and
went to the synagogue, as was his custom on the sabbath.
He stood up to read. And they gave him the scroll of the

prophet Isaiah and, when he opened it, he found the place where it was written:

> *"The spirit of [God] is upon me,*
> *because [God] has anointed me*
> *to preach good news to the poor.*
> *[God] has sent me to proclaim release to the captives,*
> *and sight to the blind;*
> *to set free those who have been oppressed,*
> *and to proclaim the acceptable year of [God]."*

And when he had rolled up the scroll, he gave it to the attendant and sat down. The eyes of everyone in the synagogue were upon him, and he began to say to them, "Today this scripture has been fulfilled in your hearing." And everyone approved of him and wondered at the gracious words that came out of his mouth and said, "Isn't this Joseph's son?" Then he said to them, "No doubt you will quote me the proverb, 'Physician, heal thyself: Do now in your own city the things we heard tell of from Capernaum.'" But he said, "Truly I tell you that no prophet is accepted in his own city. For I tell you the truth: There were many widows in Israel in Elijah's day, when the heavens were locked up for three and a half years, and there was a great famine over the whole land; but Elijah was not sent to any one of them, but to the widow woman at Zarephath in Sidon. And there were many lepers in Israel in the time of the prophet Elisha, but not one of them was cleansed—only Naaman the Syrian." And when everyone in the synagogue heard these things, they were filled with rage and drove him out to the edge of the bluff on which the city was set in order to push him off. But he escaped from the midst of them. (Luke 4:16–30)

Several features of this episode should be noted. First, everyone initially receives Jesus' interpretation of the biblical text as good news. Moreover, the content of Jesus' message on this occasion— that the time of healing, liberation, and jubilee foretold by Isaiah is now present—is simply another form of his customary message that the realm of God is at hand. This news is good because it represents the fulfillment of Israel's hopes as they have been shaped by the texts of the law and the prophets. And, as the first part of Luke's account shows, the people of Israel gathered in the Nazareth synagogue are eager to hear it.

But Jesus does not stop with his initial exegesis. The problem is not that Isaiah's words are obscure in themselves and need to be explained. If anything, they are perhaps too well known, too readily interpreted as a message of unadulterated good news for the covenant community. Jesus, as the bearer and (as he claims) guarantor of the news that these words have been fulfilled, corrects his compatriots on just this point. Yes, the realm of God is coming—but where it comes is a matter of God's grace and not of human expectation. It follows that Israel should not presume to anticipate—let alone set conditions for—where or how God's rule will manifest itself; Israel's job as the community of promise is rather to seek out and welcome God's realm wherever God determines to bring it into being.

The thrust of Jesus' message to his neighbors is clear: there is no appropriation of the gospel apart from a commitment to meet it on God's terms. These terms are inseparable from the particular social context within which God chooses to act; furthermore, that context is integral to the meaning of the gospel itself. If God chooses to reveal the acceptable year in what seems like an unacceptable place, among unacceptable people, then the faithful person's understanding of what acceptability means must change. Once again, where and how the faith is confessed proves just as important as what is said.

As Luke makes clear, the "spin" Jesus places on the news that God's realm is at hand is not popular with the people of Nazareth. Jesus reminds his hometown congregation that God's rule often has been most clearly visible outside of Israel—with the clear implication that the same will prove to be true in the present time. And while the story of Jesus' reception in the synagogue is but one episode, the idea that God is actively building the realm of heaven where we would not expect is a theme that recurs again and again throughout the four Gospels, culminating in Jesus' own trial and crucifixion. Those whom Jesus pronounces blessed are the poor (Luke 6:20), the hungry (Luke 6:21), the sorrowful (Matt. 5:4), the meek (Matt. 5:5), the hated (Luke 6:22), and the persecuted (Matt. 5:10); in short, those of least regard in society as a whole. It is they—the prostitutes, tax collectors, and other sinners—who will enter first into the realm of heaven, because they are the ones who receive it as it comes (Matt. 21:31–32; compare Luke 7:29). On the other hand, those who think they know all about God's realm (and, therefore, feel justified in demanding that Jesus reveal it on their terms) remain unmoved (Matt. 16:1–4 and pars.; compare John 9:39–41).

This repeated preference for the poor and otherwise excluded as both the sign and locus of the coming realm of God fuels a growing hostility to Jesus and his message among the established authorities both inside and outside the community of Israel. Jesus himself recognizes that his association of the realm of God with the marginalized will cause offense (Matt. 11:4–6; Luke 7:22–23), and his suspicions are amply realized. Within the faith community, it is assumed that if Jesus were truly the agent of God's rule, he would avoid contact with sinners (Luke 7:39). Yet, far from avoiding them, he consorts with them openly (Matt. 9:11 and pars.) and gains a reputation as their friend (Matt. 11:19; Luke 7:34). Given this pattern of behavior, the conclusion is quickly drawn that Jesus does not come from God, but is in fact an agent of the devil (Matt. 12:24 and pars.; compare John 8:48).

For the political authorities of Rome, outside the community of Israel, opposition to Jesus lacks this level of theological sophistication, but the issue is much the same. Jesus' activity is perceived as a threat to the established order. His confession of God, realized as solidarity with those who fall outside the established channels of power, implicitly renders the presence of God—and thus the ultimate authority that God exercises—independent of the existing structures of the *pax Romana*. Jesus thereby forces a choice between himself and Caesar that leaves no doubt as to how the constituted powers will decide his fate (John 19:12). Indeed, where Jesus is concerned, the common interest is obvious enough to foster cooperation even between two political rivals like Pilate and Herod (Luke 23:6–7, 11–12).[4]

The convergence of interest among the Jewish and Roman authorities brings Jesus' ministry to a swift end. Having taken up his position among the outcasts, Jesus becomes one himself, abandoned by all, including his own disciples. Having challenged every practice that denies to the poor and the sick full recognition as members of the covenant community, Jesus is himself denied, not only by that community's leaders but also by his closest friend (Matt. 26:69–74 and pars.). Having come so that all might have abundant life (John 10:10), he is sentenced to a shameful death. Having lived and worked at the margins of his society, he dies there—crucified outside the walls, where the garbage is thrown.[5]

In this way, Jesus' own career exemplifies the counterintuitive way in which the realm he proclaims comes into the world. Nor was this point lost on his contemporaries, who were scandalized by the implication that Jesus' own social location was a reliable indicator of where God was at work bringing God's realm into being (see, for example, Matt. 11:19; 13:53–57; 15:1–12). For as the biblical accounts of his ministry make quite clear, Jesus did not identify this spot with the center of worldly political power (Rome), with the leaders of the cult (the Saduccees), or even with the champions of popular piety (the Pharisees). He identified it rather with those on the margins of political and religious orders alike.[6] Among these "little ones," Jesus both proclaimed the reality of and found compelling evidence for God's coming rule. In this way, Jesus' confession of the God of Israel was inseparable from his speaking together with the poor and outcast. By pointing to the presence and power of God in the lives of those held to be of little account by society at large, Jesus challenged his contemporaries to recognize that God's work in history takes the form of commitment to the well-being of such people. The God proclaimed by Christ stands unequivocally with the marginalized.[7]

This certainly does not mean that Jesus confessed the marginalized as God, but it does mean that Jesus' experience of God was so closely bound up with them that solidarity with them was constitutive of his confession of God. And while Jesus proclaimed the coming of God's realm as good news for the whole of humankind, it is no more possible for us than for him to separate the social location of God's breaking into history from the character of the realm that results from this inbreaking. It follows that if we are to imitate the "good confession" of Jesus by speaking together with him, then we, too, must seek out God at the margins. Such a God does not reign "from the top down," through established channels of power and authority; instead, this God works at the periphery of society to build God's realm "from the outside in."

THE CHARACTER OF JESUS' CONFESSION

This understanding of confession is consistent with the principle that only the Jesus encountered in Scripture can instruct the community on the conditions of that encounter. Jesus Christ's identification with the community remains the basis for Christian claims to speak with authority: because the presence of Jesus as Savior is inseparable from his scripturally rendered identity, and because that identity is inseparable from (even as it redefines) the history of the covenant community, the Christian encounter with Jesus is inseparable from sharing in the life of that community.

At the same time, the Gospel accounts make it clear that nothing could be more misguided than to treat the community of faith as an undifferentiated monolith. Just as any action attributed to the community as a whole ultimately reduces to the actions of specific individuals within it, so any encounter with the community always takes the form of an encounter with specific individuals who in some way or other stand as the community's representatives. It is therefore impossible to speak meaningfully about Jesus' solidarity with the community without knowing through whom in particular that solidarity is mediated. Significantly, those with whom Jesus associates most closely are neither the leaders of Israel nor the masses of conventionally pious Jews, but with those whose status in the community is suspect (see Matt. 9:11–12; 11:19 and pars.).[8] The fact that Jesus' confession of God is in this way bound up with the practice of speaking with those on the community's margins provides this specificity and thereby says something about the way in which the God whose reign Jesus proclaims chooses to rule.

As Jesus himself points out in his sermon in Nazareth, moreover, God's concern for the outsider has ample precedent in the Old Testament history of God's dealings with Israel. While the specific examples of this divine partiality for the marginalized are many, the exodus is particularly significant given its paradigmatic status both for Israel's own self-understanding as a community and for its understanding of God.[9]

From this starting point, the motif of God's working from the outside in can be traced through a number of biblical traditions. Even those strands of the Old Testament (like those found in Isaiah and some of the Psalms) which emphasize the monarchy rather than the exodus as the decisive act in God's dealings with Israel nonetheless affirm God's special concern for the marginalized.[10] Indeed, Saul and David themselves are depicted as being somewhat unlikely candidates for Israel's throne, who were called to be kings in spite of appearances (1 Sam. 9:21; 16:1–13).[11]

In the book of Ruth, the Davidic monarchy provides the background for a particularly striking example of God's practice of shaping the covenant community from the margins. As a Moabite, Ruth's only connection to the elect community is her mother-in-law, Naomi, who, widowed and bereft of her two sons, is herself on the periphery of the patriarchally constituted Israelite society (Ruth 1:11–13). Yet Ruth casts her lot with Naomi and her community in an act of solidarity that has all the characteristics of genuine confession:

> Do not press me to leave you
> or to turn back from following you
> Where you go, I will go;
> Where you lodge, I will lodge;
> your people shall be my people,
> and your God my God.
> Where you die, I will die—
> there I will be buried.
> May [God] do thus and so to me,
> and more as well,
> if even death parts me from you! (Ruth 1:16–17)

Once in Israel, Ruth goes out to glean in the fields of Boaz, a kinsman who, much to Ruth's surprise, shows her special favor. "Why have I found favor in your sight, that you should take notice of me, when I am a foreigner?" (Ruth 2:10). Boaz cites Ruth's faithfulness to Naomi, which he interprets as not simply an act of human loyalty but a decision to join within the covenant community established by the God of Israel.

In this way, solidarity with those in distress (in this case the aged Naomi, widowed and bereft of her two sons) serves as the basis for a confession of the God of Israel: "All that you have done for your mother-in-law since the death of your husband has been fully told me, and how you left your father and mother and your native land and came to a people that you did not know before. May [God] reward you for your deeds, and may you have a full reward from . . . the God of Israel, under whose wings you have come for refuge!" (Ruth 2:11–12).

In light of this reaction, Ruth is encouraged to ask Boaz to exercise his right as next-of-kin and "redeem" her as wife, thereby assuring her (and her mother-in-law) a secure place within Israelite society. Interestingly, there is a complication at this point, for we learn of a more closely related kinsman who must first be given the chance to "redeem" Ruth. Boaz explains the situation to him:

> "Naomi, who has come back from the country of Moab,
> is selling a parcel of land that belonged to our kinsman
> Elimelech. So I thought I would tell you of it, and say: Buy
> it in the presence of those sitting here, and in the presence
> of the elders of my people. If you will redeem it, redeem it;
> but if you will not, tell me, so that I may know; for there is
> no one prior to you to redeem it, and I come after you."
> So he said, "I will redeem it." Then Boaz said, "The day
> you acquire the field from the hand of Naomi, you are also
> acquiring Ruth the Moabite, the widow of the dead man,
> to maintain the dead man's inheritance." At this, the next-
> of-kin said, "I cannot redeem it for myself without damag-
> ing my own inheritance. Take my right of redemption
> yourself, for I cannot redeem it." (Ruth 4:3–6)

So long as redemption involved only property, the kinsman is eager to exercise his right; but as soon as it is revealed to involve risk to his own status (by the dilution of his own wealth through the assumption of responsibility for the dead man's family), he declines. Ironically, the name of this man, so intent on maintaining the integrity of his patrimony, is forgotten. Boaz, however, is remembered, for he had a child by Ruth, who, in turn, "became the father of Jesse, the father of David" (Ruth 4:17). In this way, the story of Ruth provides a classic illustration of the principle that speaking with (and thus taking on the story of) another provides the basis for the preservation of one's own story before God.

The fact that this account of David's non-Israelite roots prefaces the whole subsequent history of the monarchy stands as an elegant witness to the idea that the biblical God builds the community "from the outside in." This pattern of divine activity is not the only one to which Scripture bears witness; indeed, it owes much of its effect to the fact that it stands in tension with more exclusivist traditions prominent at other places in the Old Testament. The Deuteronomic code, for example, forbids intermarriage with other peoples and explicitly excludes Moabites from the community (Deut. 7:1–4; 23:3). And the theme of Ruth certainly accords ill with the witness of Ezra and Nehemiah, for whom the practice of marrying foreign women was decisive evidence of Israel's faithlessness (Ezra 10:2, 10–14; Neh. 13:23–27).

Yet while these other traditions are forcible reminders that God's work at the margins stands in tension with an equally biblical affirmation of the communal center, the persistence with which the socially, religiously, or politically insignificant are chosen as instruments of divine activity (see, for example, Gen. 17:15–21; Judg. 6:14–16; 1 Sam. 1:1–28; Jer. 1:6–10; Amos 7:14–15) suggests that the community's periphery holds peculiar significance in the economy of salvation.

This supposition finds definitive confirmation in the story of Jesus, in whom, according to Christian confession, the center and the margins coincide, insofar as the presence of the one who was crucified is also confessed as the Son of David (Matt. 1:1–20; 9:27; 15:23; 21:9, 15 and pars.). In this context, it is altogether appropriate that Jesus should pick up the theme of Ruth by suggesting that God's work of building the community may extend beyond the boundaries of Israel (Matt. 8:5–13; Luke 7:2–10; compare Matt. 15:21–28; Mark 7:24–30; Luke 4:24–28).

THE IDENTITY OF THOSE WHOM JESUS CONFESSES

Through the fact that he preaches the coming of God's realm from the outside in, Jesus' confession reveals a division within the covenant community (see Luke 2:34). On one side are the poor, the sinners, and the demon-possessed; on the other are the scribes, the Pharisees, and the priestly class of Saduccees. Jesus proclaims the advent of God's realm to both groups, but the connection between what Jesus says about God's realm and the place from which he says it dictates that the meaning of this proclamation (and, consequently, its reception) vary with the audience.

For the outcasts, it is a proclamation of divine favor to all who would be reconciled to God: to them apply the parables of the lost sheep, the lost coin, and the prodigal son (Luke 15:3–32). For those invested with power and prestige, God's realm comes in the form of judgment, revealing their unwillingness to meet God on God's own terms: against them are spoken the parables of the marriage feast (Matt. 22:1–10; Luke 14:15–24), the murderous tenants (Matt. 21:33–41 and pars.), and the unforgiving debtor (Matt. 18:23–34).

Granted that Jesus' identification with the marginalized is decisive for understanding the content as well as the form of his message, however, the meaning of "solidarity with the marginalized" needs to be filled out in more detail before it can function as a criterion of the good confession among Christians. In this context, the chief point to be made is that because Jesus is the ultimate object of Christian confession, the demand for "solidarity with the marginalized" is theologically justifiable only insofar as it points to Jesus. Loosed from the person of Jesus, "solidarity with the oppressed"— like "justification by grace through faith"—reduces to an abstraction that is incapable of maintaining genuine critical purchase over a church that remains all too easily tempted to take Jesus' place as the bearer and guarantor of salvation.

So when we ask what God's active presence among the marginalized means for those who confess Jesus, it is necessary to recognize that the Gospel narratives themselves limit the number of generalizations that can be made about the identity of the marginalized. Moreover, what patterns do emerge in the New Testament find their coherence only with reference to the larger story of Jesus, into which they are woven.

Taking these cautionary points into account, it nonetheless remains the case that in the Gospels Jesus is seen most clearly for who he is not by the twelve disciples but by a series of shadowy, largely nameless characters who break the surface of the story only to sink once again into obscurity once their moment is past.[12] Not only do these figures (who thus sit on the margins of the narrative as well as of society at large) seem to have a special capacity to recognize Jesus; they are also the ones in relation to whom Jesus' own identity comes most sharply into relief.[13]

When we seek to describe these marginalized characters more specifically, it turns out that their sociological characteristics are anything but uniform. The majority are Jewish, and thus they stand within (even if on the margins of) the covenant community. Yet while Jesus does on one occasion explicitly restrict his mission to Israel (Matt. 10:5–6; but compare 28:19–20 and John 10:16), a significant subset of "marginal" characters comes from beyond Israel's boundaries, among the despised communities of Samaritans and (Roman) Gentiles.[14] These figures, too, play a crucial role in the rendering of Jesus' identity, even if their significance is dependent upon their location within the broader history of Israel of which the Gospel narratives are part (John 4:22).

An airtight definition of the margins within which Jesus lives and moves is thus difficult to formulate. What is clear is that the marginalized do not occupy recognized positions of authority within the covenant community. This fact distances them not only from the established Jewish leadership, but also from the twelve disciples, whose frequent incomprehension contrasts markedly with the often exemplary faith of more marginal characters.[15] In this way, the evangelists suggest that the disciples' importance lies less in their theological brilliance than in the continuity of their witness to Jesus. As the communal center of the church, the disciples and those who succeed them function as the guardians and the interpreters of Jesus' confession for the community as a whole. The marginalized do not have this community-shaping role, even though they may be theologically more perceptive than (and thereby provide a necessary corrective to) the disciples in particular situations.

Although the marginalized are rather ephemeral characters in the Gospels, it would be a mistake to conclude that their theological significance is limited to the beginning of the Christian movement and ceases later on. Jesus continually drags his disciples to the margins, against their will and even their understanding. Moreover, his insistence on bearing the cross (Matt. 16:24 and pars.), on the need of the greatest in the community to be a servant (Matt. 20:25–28 and pars.; John 13:12–17), and on God's special care for the "little ones" (Matt. 18:6–7, 10) makes it clear that the disciples' movement to the margins is to continue even after Pentecost.[16]

To summarize, the "marginalized" in the New Testament are best understood as those who are removed from recognized positions of power in the covenant community. Generally (though, as the story of Zacchaeus shows, not necessarily), these persons command a disproportionately small share of the material and political capital of the society of which they are a part. Such status is obviously not limited to church members, and in his great eschatological discourse (Matt. 25), Jesus makes no connection at all between his solidarity with the marginalized and their own faith commitments. Furthermore, although some texts do portray Jesus' mission in a decidedly exclusivist light (for example, Matt. 10:6), the traditional boundaries of the covenant community ultimately seem incapable of circumscribing the power of the gospel he proclaims (see especially Matt. 15:21–28; Acts 10:34–48).

However diverse their backgrounds may be, the Bible's marginal characters acquire theological significance only as they are brought within the cultural-linguistic context of Jesus' proclamation. It is the command and example of Jesus that lead those at the church's center (exemplified in the Gospel narratives by the disciples) to the margins, and only by constant reference to Jesus does this drive to the margins maintain its distinctive shape.

Yet the importance of this logical distinction between the person of Jesus and the social context within which his character takes shape should not be allowed to obscure the fact that in the biblical narrative the two are inseparable. That God should be revealed in this way may be understood formally as a matter of divine freedom; but the church has no ground for using this distinction to distance itself from the margins without being false to the God who took flesh in the person of Jesus of Nazareth.

Nor should the cost of living at the margins be minimized. The margins are fundamentally a place of abandonment. Socially, a person is defined by his or her relationship to established centers of power and prestige. Existence at the margins constitutes a social dislocation profound enough to threaten one's very status as a human being within a community. Consequently, the marginalized serve as a potent reminder of the precariousness of a person's place within the social order.

Indeed, precisely to the extent that they are removed from positions of respectability, the marginalized can seem in their very persons a threat to the structures that give a society its form and stability. It is therefore not surprising that marginal status is often interpreted by those at the center as a sign of judgment: because those at the periphery have evidently been abandoned by the God who grounds and guarantees the social order, they are rightfully abandoned by the community as well.[17]

Apart from the context provided by the story of Jesus, the act of identifying with such people is quite naturally interpreted as a symptom of insanity or malevolence.[18] Yet the biblical identification of the crucified Jesus with the risen Savior implies that the apparent abandonment by God experienced by those at the margins is in fact the point at which God draws closest to the human condition. The suffering that otherwise would be a cause for despair and a mark of defeat becomes bearable in hope to the extent that it is lived out of the Christian proclamation of God's presence among the least. It follows that Christians are not called to the margins out of some romantic idea that life there is ennobling, but simply because the margins are where Jesus Christ is to be found and thus the matrix within which the gospel message acquires its full sense and power. Indeed, if the witness of Scripture is taken seriously, it is possible to go so far as to say that the proclamation of Jesus Christ is gospel only when spoken at the margins.

THE COMPLEMENTARITY OF MARGINS AND CENTER

According to the biblical witness, this last point—that the proclamation of Jesus Christ is gospel only when spoken at the margins—was not lost on the first generation of Jesus' disciples. The church in Jerusalem was evidently defined by its commitment to poverty (Rom. 15:26; Gal. 2:10; compare Acts 2:44). And while Paul does not share the evangelists' focus on the physical conditions of Jesus' ministry, in his thought the role of the margins in determining the character of God's rule is all but elevated to the status of an ecclesiological principle:

> Look at your own calling, brothers and sisters: for not many
> of you were wise by worldly standards, not many of you
> were powerful, not many of noble birth. But God chose
> the foolish of this world to shame the wise, and God chose
> what is weak in the world to shame the strong, and God
> chose what is despised as of no account in the world, even
> what is not, in order to confound what is, so that no one
> might boast before God. (1 Cor. 1:26–29; compare Matt.
> 9:25–26 and pars.; James 2:5)

God's practice of building the community from the outside in is here interpreted as a sociological corollary to the idea of justification by grace. A similar perspective is evident in the faith of African American slave Christians, who sang, "I sought . . . my Lord in de wilderness, in de wilderness, in de wilderness," and then continued in the second verse, "I found . . . grace in de wilderness."[19] Because only the community that allows itself to be built from the margins gives substance to the claim that it lives entirely by grace, a truly Christian community is obliged to pursue an existence on the margins.

This having been said, however, it remains the case that Jesus does not simply undercut the authority of the community's established leadership. In this respect, his solidarity with the community as a whole includes those in positions of power. While Gospel writers are certainly not reluctant to admit that the community's leaders can prove unfaithful to their mandate, they implicitly acknowledge the role of the leadership in preserving the broader tradition upon which even Jesus' own critiques of current practice depend for their coherence and force.[20] Thus, even though Jesus is critical of the practice of Israel's leaders, he is quick to acknowledge their role as guarantors of the covenantal tradition, within which he situates himself (Matt. 23:2–3; compare v. 23). The point is thus not that the priests, scribes, and Pharisees lack authority in principle, but that in practice they prove unable to use their position to discern the presence of God in their midst (Luke 13:34; compare Matt. 23:29–34). Specifically, they fail to understand that the God whose authority they rightly seek to claim does not work from the top down, but from the outside in.

Although the Old Testament offers significant examples of this outside-in direction of community building, Jesus is for Christians the defining instance of this way of God's working. And because Jesus is who he is, if Christians ground their claim to speak with authority in Jesus' relationship to the church, then they cannot simply rest with the fact of Jesus' commitment to the community without being impelled to examine the nature of that commitment.

The fact that the Gospel rendering of Jesus' identity is inseparable from the broader story of the covenant community gives the community (the traditions of which may be preserved in oral or written form) a critical role in shaping the Christian reading of Scripture. But the corresponding fact, no less central to the Gospel narratives, that Jesus confronts—and thereby defines—that community from the periphery suggests that it is from the church's fringes that the presence of Jesus will continue to make itself felt in the ongoing history of the community. Consequently, the authority of the community cannot simply be identified with the authority of its leaders, even if it is there that the community as a whole finds its functional center of gravity.

Jesus' solidarity with the community is thus no basis for the subsuming of individual identity under the will of the collective as defined by the church's established authorities. On the contrary, if the fact of Jesus' identification with the community grounds the authority Christians claim for their reading of Scripture, the mode of that identification demands that the individual believer—precisely insofar as he or she is *distant* from the consensus defined and promoted by those at the center—be recognized, at least potentially, as the means by which the priority of Scripture (and, by extension, the sovereignty of Jesus) over the collective is realized concretely. This does not mean that those nearer the center are necessarily to be cast in the role of Pharisees, but it does mean that they will avoid such associations only to the extent that they prove willing to be challenged by voices from the edge.

Openness to the challenge of distant voices should not be confused with unconditioned receptivity to every wind of new doctrine that blows through the church (see Eph. 4:14ff.). A position at the periphery is no more a guarantee of Christian faithfulness than one at the center; but because the leadership of the community is the focal point for its institutional identity, it is on the leaders in particular that the demand for openness to novel interpretations of Scripture (and to whatever reform of practice they may imply) rests.

In this way, the internal sociological differentiation of the faith community provides the basis for the idea that the church is to be identified not only by the orthodoxy of what it says, but by the orthopraxy of how it comes to say it; not only by correctness of speech, but also by its willingness to listen. And for those on the periphery, the converse is true: they must display not only a willingness to listen to the consensus established at the center, but also be willing to challenge it in speech. In the words of Leonardo Boff, the community as a whole is called to be both *ecclesia discens* and *ecclesia docens.*[21]

This coupling of orthopraxy with orthodoxy rules out any doctrinal triumphalism in which proclamation is viewed simply as the handing on of a fixed *depositum fidei,* the content of which is guaranteed by the institutional or confessional integrity of the faith community. At the same time, given a belief in the priority and sufficiency of Scripture as the source of knowledge of the God of Jesus Christ, any plausible list of marks of the church will certainly include a doctrinal component.

As shown in chapter 4, the principle of *sola Scriptura* presupposes certain beliefs regarding the faithfulness of God and the ultimacy of Jesus which function as general hermeneutical constraints on the Christian reading of Scripture. Insofar as doctrinal criteria come to be enforced by the community's established authorities, however, they appear to leave little room for the kind of criticism of the community's practices that the Scripture principle was formulated to defend. This apparent inconsistency is resolved only when the nature of the community's claim to authority is examined in terms of its source in the narratively rendered identity of Jesus.

Such analysis suggests that the submission of the community to the witness of Scripture is realized concretely in its openness to the interpretive proposals of individuals removed from the centers of authority, since Jesus' own way of expressing solidarity with the community in the Gospels (and thus investing it with authority in the first place) is through his identification with such individuals. In line with these observations, the character of a good confession may be described concretely as a matter of speaking the gospel from the margins in fidelity to the biblical rendering of Jesus' (and thus the community's) identity.

Once again, this does not mean that there is no place for an established center of authority in the church, since some commonly recognized set of "official" structures is necessary if the authority bequeathed to the church is to be held accountable to the community as a whole.[22] For while God stands over against the whole church, including its leaders, God's commitment to the church cannot be separated from the work of those leaders as those who have been regularly called to proclaim Scripture as God's Word.

At the same time, because divine priority does include the church's leaders, "it is necessary to obey God rather than human beings" (Acts 5:29) when those leaders prove faithless to the gospel they have been called to proclaim. Moreover, because encounter with the marginalized defined the content of Jesus' own preaching as gospel, the authority of those holding positions of leadership in the church can be measured specifically by their willingness to subvert their own privileged status in openness to the voices of those on the margins.

The center must serve as the principal addressee of the marginalized if their witness is to shape that of the community as a whole.[23] Just as the center, as the locus of "official" teaching in the church, must always look to the periphery as the horizon where God's Word appears as gospel, the periphery is called to speak to the center as the place where that gospel takes official and permanent form.[24]

The interdependence of the periphery and the center means that the church is an authoritative community only insofar as it is also a responsible community. In a way, this conclusion is hardly surprising, since the whole concept of "marks" against which a community's claim to be the church may be evaluated makes sense only if the community can be held responsible to some standard. The challenge is how to set up such a standard without simply undermining any claim to authority the church might make.

While there may be general agreement within the church that the community of faith is accountable to God and, more specifically, to the witness of Scripture, it proves difficult to avoid logical tangles when trying to explain just how this priority functions in practice. Nor can this problem be solved simply by setting the witness of individuals against that of the church, since individuals exist as Christians only in the church. Consequently, one cannot hope as a Christian to find a theological foothold outside the church from which to stand in judgment over it. That is why it is important to speak in terms of responsibility, because a relationship of responsibility implies a shared cultural-linguistic framework: one is not responsible to a person or group whose claims one does not recognize.[25] If evaluation of communal practice is to respect the community's role in regulating that practice, it must take place in a context of commitment to the life of the community as a whole.[26]

Nevertheless, nothing could be more dangerous than to interpret the idea of mutual responsibility in terms of an equal balance between center and periphery. On the contrary, the kind of responsibility suggested by the Gospel portrait of Jesus demands a definite *im*balance in which it is necessary to adopt a "preferential option for the poor." History makes it clear that any theology that fails to privilege the marginalized will invariably privilege the center, insofar as the church's established practices (precisely insofar as they *are* established) already reflect its existing relations of power and influence.

Even where there is no explicit policy of excluding marginalized groups from positions of leadership, the community's accepted criteria of rationality and objectivity (not to mention access to media where they can be debated) are likely to be closely enough intertwined with the prevailing social organization to leave the marginalized little cultural leverage to challenge established practices.[27] Consequently, if there is truly to be mutual responsibility between the church's center and margins, the former must make a deliberate effort to marginalize itself in order to create conditions under which existing structures can be challenged. That no corresponding sacrifice of position is asked from the marginalized simply reflects the fact that they (by definition) have no position to sacrifice. Their responsibility to the center is effectively fulfilled to the extent that they continue to participate in the church and, in so doing, acknowledge Scripture's authority in spite of the fact that the community organized around those Scriptures has relegated them to its periphery.

Within the broader context provided by Jesus' "option for the poor," a model of mutual responsibility between the church's center and its periphery provides a conceptual framework within which the criteria of orthodoxy and orthopraxy may be understood as complementary marks of the church. Each set of criteria has its place in a community that takes seriously both the fact of God's identification with the church and the mode by which that identification takes place, for it is Scripture's testimony that Jesus who, by identifying with the community, grounds the authority of its leadership does so from the community's periphery, thereby undercutting any claim of the leadership to be either theologically or sociologically self-sufficient.

Insofar as the criterion of orthodoxy takes the form of confessional statements that are enforced by the community's leadership, it amounts to a call to the periphery to be responsible to the center. Those on the margins are challenged to affirm solidarity with the community as a whole by acknowledging the role of the center as both the precipitate and goal of God's work of building the church as a community of witness.

By contrast, insofar as the criterion of orthopraxy reflects the fact that the confessional stance of the center is always *norma normata* and never *norma normans,* it highlights the need for the center to be responsible to the periphery by respecting the fact that God builds the community from the outside in. The community as a whole is thus responsible to God (and therefore possessed of its proper authority) only as its center and periphery are responsible to each other. Ecclesial responsibility is therefore not a matter of setting the individual against the community, but of individuals in the community being conscious of their responsibility to one another. This exercise of responsibility, in turn, serves as the means by which God through Scripture calls the church together.

In this way, both the priority of God and the integrity of the individual turn out to be compatible with recognition of theology's ecclesiocentric dimension. When formulated in terms of the Reformation doctrine of *sola Scriptura,* God's priority appears to stand in unavoidable tension with the community's role in shaping a specifically Christian reading of Scripture. While this immediate difficulty can be overcome by showing that Scripture itself implicates the community in the process of scriptural interpretation, the degree of identification between God and the community suggested by this solution appears to rob the principle of divine priority of any practical force as a test of communal practice. Yet this difficulty can be resolved if the community is willing to follow through on its own emphasis on the primacy of Scripture's content.

Underlying the *fact* of God's identification with the community's destiny lies the *way* in which that identification is effected through the life, death, and resurrection of Jesus of Nazareth. Insofar as Jesus identifies with the community through its marginalized members (and thus shapes its identity from the outside in), he establishes an intracommunal dialectic according to which the God who in Scripture calls the church into existence also through Scripture: (1) calls the community's center to keep itself open to the divine presence on its periphery, and (2) calls those on the periphery to be faithful to God's past church-forming activity as it has crystallized at the center.

The priority of God *over* the church thus takes concrete shape in the mutual responsibility of individual believers *within* the church, so that it is through the encounter of individuals with the gospel message that the community is formed and sustained as the necessary medium of that encounter. As the mode by which the church is constituted as the community of Jesus Christ, mutual responsibility can be characterized as the basic condition for the church's teaching with authority.

chapter six

THE GROUND OF AUTHORITY IN
THE DIVINE LIFE

The church's authority is grounded in its commitment to Jesus Christ and therefore in its willingness to share Jesus' commitment to the marginalized. Specifically, I have proposed: (1) that the human work of defining and regulating the community of faith, insofar as it claims divine sanction, must reflect God's exercise of authority as manifested in Jesus' ministry, and (2) that this exercise of authority works "from the outside in," as God builds the community from its margins in a way that subjects established centers of authority to an ongoing process of critique. This two-tier assertion is consistent with the witness of Scripture, inasmuch as the divine subversion of established centers of authority in the covenant community, along with the marginal status of those who speak for God in the community, is a recurring motif within the biblical narrative that achieves especially profound expression in the person of the crucified Jesus.

THE RELATIONSHIP BETWEEN THE CENTER AND THE PERIPHERY

The biblical focus on the margins is not altogether unambiguous. The so-called Zion traditions of the Old Testament celebrate the glory of Israel's monarchy. And our own reflections on the problem of theological authority began with the observation that Jesus himself "taught them as one having authority" (Matt. 7:29). To be sure, Jesus assumes this role in opposition to the established centers of religious authority represented by the scribes and Pharisees. But by claiming authority at all Jesus implicitly sets himself up as the center of a competing system of authority, with all its sociological ramifications (including an inner circle of disciples who stand closer to this new center than the large crowds who also follow Jesus).

In this context, it is important to recognize that Jesus' own exercise of authority is hardly characterized by a uniform openness to other points of view. In the Sermon on the Mount in particular, he speaks with a finality that no scribe would have dared. With his refrain, "You have heard that it was said . . . but I say to you" (Matt. 5:21–22, 27–28, 31–32, 33–34, 38–39, 43–44), Jesus sounds as if he is correcting the Torah, which would amount to his placing himself on the same level as God.[1] To the extent that this assumption of divine authority seems to put Jesus beyond the reach of human critique, it becomes difficult to specify exactly how his exercise of authority is to be distinguished from that of his opponents.

One way of addressing this problem is to argue that Jesus' attitudes toward the constituted authorities of his day simply warns against equating a person's theological authority with his or her social standing. Yet the sociological dynamics of communal practice would seem to render this kind of distinction between status and authority precarious at best. After all, no matter how closely one may wish to identify with the margins, the very act of claiming authority implicitly defines a new sociological center, with a corresponding relocation of the margins. Nor (as Jesus' own defense of those in positions of authority makes clear) is the creation of such centers objectionable in itself.

Insofar as the theological significance of the margins is bound up with the preaching of the gospel, and insofar as this preaching depends on the faithful transmission of the gospel's content, the presence of a coherent center is every bit as integral to the integrity of the church as commitment to the margins. Even if it is conceded that the content of the gospel message is inseparable from solidarity with the marginalized, it is no less true that all talk of the margins presupposes reference to a more or less well-defined center (and therefore some degree of identification with the community defined by that center). Following this line of reasoning, chapter 5 ended with the suggestion that the church's exercise of authority requires a relationship of mutual responsibility between the center and the margins.

The question is whether this model of mutuality can in practice amount to anything more than a sellout to the status quo. It is, after all, not especially controversial to acknowledge that Jesus identifies with those on the periphery of the faith community. It may even be conceded that it is Jesus' act of speaking with the marginalized that creates the conditions for the disciples' confession of Jesus. When all is said and done, however, it seems that we are left with a situation in which those at the center—the apostles and their successors in the churches—call the shots. Insofar as they define the center, a community's leaders exercise de facto control over what counts as correct doctrine. Given this basic datum of social organization, theoretical distinctions between the established practices of the church and the will of God in Jesus Christ risk fading into practical insignificance.

While this risk is real, it can be realized only if the church fails to take seriously the interdependence of the center and margins in Jesus' own ministry. If it is true that as a matter of sociological definition, all talk of the margins presupposes the ability to identify the center, it is no less the case that as a matter of theological definition, the center of the church of Jesus Christ cannot be identified independently of its commitment to the margins. In other words, the church's center—like the gospel it is charged with proclaiming—is recognizable as such only after the fact, in light of its encounter with the margins. And this, in turn, means that the goal of the theology is not (as the Reformers thought) to find a fixed point (for example, Scripture) from which to assume a theologically secure position over against the church, since even Jesus occupied no such position.

On the contrary, a position of authority modeled on that of Jesus will be characterized by mobility, in which theological security is found only through relinquishing it in an ongoing pilgrimage to the margins (see Matt. 16:25 and pars.). After all, the authority of the biblical Jesus is no more self-evident to his contemporaries than that of the church that confesses him has been to subsequent generations. Jesus' identity, like that of the church, is fleshed out against that peculiar background of supporting characters and circumstances that constitute his story. In this story, Jesus' confession of God's presence at the margins of the covenant community defines the nature of his authority quite specifically and renders theologically unpersuasive any attempt to equate that which is spoken at political center of the church with the gospel. What is spoken at the center is certainly theologically significant, since the center—whether faithful or unfaithful to its calling—remains the focal point for discourse in the community as a whole. But whether what the center says is gospel can be determined only in light of its effects at the margins.

This point is illustrated the story of the Reverend Jones's missionary sermon to African American slaves (chapter 2). Insofar as it was delivered by a professionally trained, white clergyman under the auspices of the slave masters, Jones's sermon was a product of American Christianity's center. Yet its status as gospel was tested in terms of its effects at the margins, among the slaves to whom it simply was not heard as the good news of Jesus Christ. We may suppose the sermon to have been preached with all good will (and it is worth pointing out that, racist though he was, Jones did recognize a moral obligation to preach to slaves); it was also heard with good will—and found wanting.

Given an ecclesiology based on the notion of reciprocity between the center and the margins, there is nothing particularly surprising or shameful about the views of an official representative of the church being challenged in this way. Because the evangelical character of Christian proclamation cannot be evaluated apart from its effects among the marginalized, theological errors may remain hidden until brought to light in the act of proclamation. It follows that Jones's real shortcomings as a minister of the gospel do not lie primarily in his failure on a given occasion to communicate the good news of Jesus Christ to his slave hearers, but in his refusal to take their negative reaction as a stimulus for reevaluating the content of his message.

Jones's experience serves as a warning that even those with the best ecclesiastical credentials cannot take the faithfulness of their proclamation for granted. Nor is the need for theological self-correction illustrated by Jones's preaching simply the result of fallible human beings' inability to grasp the fullness of the divine will. By itself, human fallibility is an inadequate justification of the need for critique within the church, for it leads either to an authoritarianism by default (on the grounds that strict adherence to tradition is the only way to safeguard the faith against the introduction of human error) or to a sterile relativism (in which the possibility of error leads to the conclusion that no theological position can be regarded as genuinely authoritative). The slaves' reaction to Jones's sermon is theologically compelling because it comes from the margins, and Jesus himself makes it clear that the gospel's status as good news is closely bound to its reception as such by the marginalized. Nor do the marginalized have this significance because of a fundamental discontinuity between the (infallible) divine and (fallible) human spheres; on the contrary, it is rooted in a basic *continuity* between the situation of the church and that of the God who in Jesus Christ took on the finite conditions of human life. Indeed, the fact that in Jesus Christ the identity of God no less than that of the church is bound up with the marginalized means that no one, *including Jesus himself,* may be regarded as having theological authority apart from commitment to the marginalized.

I take this last assertion, or some version of it, to be the fundamental contention of the many theologies that characterize themselves as liberationist. Often, such theologies are opposed by more traditional Christian thinkers on the ground that this willingness to make even the confession of Jesus relative to the fate of the marginalized represents a fundamental betrayal of Christian faith. As noted earlier, in the context of examining the position of James Cone, it is not the case that liberation theologians necessarily undermine the priority of Christ.[2] Indeed, the logic of their position is arguably close to that of Paul when he writes, "I pray that I might be cursed before Christ for the sake of my brothers and sisters, my compatriots according to the flesh" (Rom. 9:3).

Paul is certainly not implying that life with Christ is only a relative good; on the contrary, his expression of the wish to be cursed reflects the degree of his commitment to Jesus, who became accursed for our sakes (see Gal. 3:13). From this perspective, commitment to the basic insights of liberation theology need not involve elevating the marginalized over Jesus Christ. On the contrary, it means to recognize that, in light of the fact that Jesus binds his own identity as the Christ to his work among the marginalized, one's commitment to Jesus is finally measured by one's commitment to the marginalized.

Humanly compelling though Jesus' own "preferential option for the poor" may be, however, it cannot be regarded as decisive for all subsequent exercise of authority in the church unless God's own identity and authority are at stake in Jesus' ministry. While it is possible to see inchoate forms of this claim within the New Testament, its full implications for Christian faith were worked out only with the definition of the dogma of the Trinity.

The fact that the church's adoption of trinitarian doctrine was mired in the often sordid ecclesiastical politics of the late Roman Empire might seem to militate against the likelihood of its compatibility with the thesis that genuine authority moves from the outside in. And yet the doctrine of the Trinity has increasingly found defenders among theologians with liberationist concerns. Justo Gonzalez argues that the Trinity serves as a model for human social organization,[3] since "faith in the Crucified One who is 'of one substance with the Father,' has enormous liberating and subversive power [because it] is faith in a God who joins the dispossessed in their struggle and marches with them to victory liberation and new life."[4] In similar fashion, Patricia Wilson-Kastner claims trinitarian mutuality for feminist theological discourse,[5] while Leonardo Boff gives perhaps the most detailed development of this theme in his book-length analysis of the social implications of trinitarian doctrine.[6]

But while all three writers take note of God's solidarity with the marginalized in Jesus Christ, none connects this "preferential option for the poor" directly to the trinitarian structure of divine life. This is not to suggest that any of these theologians compromises the divinity of Jesus, but only to point out that for them, God's (economic) activity in Jesus Christ appears to be logically independent of God's own (immanent) life of communion. Gonzalez, Wilson-Kastner, and Boff all seem to conceive God's intra-trinitarian existence as a mutuality devoid of internal distinctions. Consequently, while all three writers are staunch defenders of the principle that God works from the margins, they stop short of the idea that the ecclesiological interdependence of the margins and the center is rooted in the inner structure of God's own life.

A more promising appropriation of trinitarian doctrine can be found in the work of the Catholic feminist theologian Catherine Mowry LaCugna. While quite cognizant of the ways in which trinitarian language has been used to further the cause of patriarchy in the churches,[7] LaCugna couples a feminist hermeneutics of suspicion with a hermeneutics of retrieval that sees in trinitarian doctrine a powerful challenge to patriarchy in the church. Although she is appreciative of the efforts of those who see in the Trinity a pattern for human social organization, LaCugna suggests that the approaches of Wilson-Kastner and Boff reflect a Western, Augustinian-Thomistic emphasis on the ontological priority of the (one) divine substance over the (three) divine persons that decouples trinitarian language from the particulars of salvation history and thereby leaves its proponents open to the charge of having simply projected their own political sensibilities onto the Godhead.

LaCugna argues that this pitfall can be avoided by turning instead to the resources of Orthodox trinitarian theology, which, as developed by the Cappadocians, roots God's unity in the distinct operations of the divine persons in history.[8] That is, if it is true that Jesus' practice in particular can be decisive for Christians only insofar as it can be rooted in God's own being, then it must also be true that all talk about who and how God is must be rooted in Jesus' career.

As will be made clear in what follows, attention to the details of this career demand the recognition that the triune God is not an undifferentiated community of persons, but a life characterized by a definite internal ordering of distinct ministries. At the same time, this order need not be interpreted in terms of a hierarchy, in which the divine persons exist in a relationships of super- and subordination. On the contrary (and as the Cappadocians themselves insisted), the logic of the biblical narrative militates against the idea that any one of the divine persons is in any way subordinate to another.

Following LaCugna's lead, I will attempt to show that the confessional approach to theology proposed in chapter 5 is rooted in the fact that God, too, lives from the margins, and that the doctrine of the Trinity entails just that claim. As may be expected, this proposal requires viewing Jesus' movement to the margins as not only reflective but actually constitutive of God's own distinctive way of being. Without some such connection between the internal life of the Godhead and the social dynamics of Jesus' ministry, the plausibility of attributing ultimate significance to Jesus' story (including its defining sociopolitical features) seems questionable at best. After all, if God's own being is not fully disclosed in Jesus' career, then it seems necessary to admit that Jesus—and the good news he proclaims—may not be God's final word to humankind.

But if in Jesus' ministry we indeed confront the very heart of God, then it seems incumbent upon Christians to explain exactly what sort of God is able both to be in Jesus and, in some sense, distinct from him as the one whose reign Jesus proclaims. Whether the doctrine of Trinity is the most satisfactory way of coming to terms with who Jesus is remains to be seen. The need for some such account, however, seems beyond question if Christian claims about Jesus' authority (let alone that of the church) are to be defended against the charge of arbitrariness.

THE MUTUAL CONFESSION OF THE FATHER AND THE SON

Confession, as noted in chapter 5, refers to the act of speaking with another. Christian confession, as the source and medium of Christian claims to speak with authority, is based on a commitment to speak with Jesus—a commitment that is inseparable from speaking together with the marginalized members of the faith community who are the locus of Jesus' own earthly ministry. And yet, at least initially, the characterization of Jesus' life in terms of confession seems to divert attention from this commitment; for while the marginalized are the context for Jesus' "good confession," God is its object.

This fact seems to reaffirm a basic distinction between the confession of God, on one hand, and commitment to the marginalized, on the other. These two aspects of Jesus' ministry can be brought together only if Jesus' speaking together with God is so intimate that one's response to Jesus' own person (including especially his solidarity with the poor) is functionally equivalent to one's response to the God whose reign Jesus proclaims. According to the evangelists, Jesus makes just such a claim about himself: "The one who believes in me does not believe in me, but in the one who sent me; and the one who sees me sees the one who sent me" (John 12:44–45; compare 14:9–11; Mark 9:37). Given this functional equality between Jesus and the God he proclaims, there is no longer any criterion of divine identity that one might invoke over against the person and practice of Jesus. Jesus himself has become the basic criterion of who God is.

The intimacy of Jesus' relationship with God is displayed most concretely in his practice of addressing God as Father (Matt. 11:25; Mark 14:36; John 5:17 and passim). In the Gospels, this term does not function as a general description of the relationship between God and humankind; on the contrary, the evangelists insist that "no one knows the Father except the Son" (Matt. 11:27; Luke 11:22; compare John 1:18).[9] Indeed, Jesus' confession of God as Father provides at least a preliminary rationale for the Christian confession of Jesus. Even though Jesus' confession entails his pointing away from himself, the fact that the one to whom he points he calls "Father" illuminates his own status as the Son.[10] In other words, the intimate character of his relationship to the Father is such that the same act of confession through which Jesus distinguishes himself from God (see, for example, John 14:28) also implies his profound unity with God (see John 10:30; 14:9–11).

And yet if it is truly the case that Jesus so closely identifies his will (John 6:38), teaching (John 7:16), works (John 9:4), and words (John 14:24) with God that to reject Jesus is equivalent to rejecting God (Luke 10:16), it is natural to ask on what basis such seemingly extravagant claims are to be believed. The evangelists suggest that belief in Jesus as the true confessor of the God of Israel is justified because this same God also confesses Jesus. Jesus' witness is not meant to be understood as self-authenticating; it is authentic because the God he calls Father bears witness to it (John 5:37).

This witness is mediated in a number of ways, including the works of power that Jesus performs (John 5:36; 10:25) and which are generally accepted by Jesus' contemporaries as evidence of supernatural power (see, for example, Mark 1:27; 7:37; Matt. 8:27 and pars.; John 2:11; 4:64; 6:2; 9:16; 11:47). In any case, Jesus himself cites the works he does in support of the authenticity of his message (Matt. 9:1–8 and pars.; John 10:38). Indeed, in response to the charge that he casts out devils in the devil's name, Jesus counters that the content of his miracles testifies to their divine origin: the fact that the forces of evil are set to flight is sufficient evidence of the fact that the power of God is at work (Matt. 12:22–29 and pars.).

Impressive witness though the miracles may be, however, they do not themselves elevate Jesus above the level of the prophets, who also worked wonders, including the resuscitation of the dead (see 1 Kings 17:17–24). Yet God's vindication of Jesus' ministry is not limited to the indirect witness of the miracles. It also takes the explicitly confessional form of speaking. At Jesus' baptism, the inauguration of his public ministry, there comes "a voice from heaven saying, 'This is my beloved Son, with whom I am well pleased'" (Matt. 3:17 and pars.; compare John 1:32–33). The same words sound again at the Transfiguration, with the added injunction, "Listen to him!" (Matt. 17:5 and pars.). And finally, as Jesus' ministry nears its climax, God speaks yet once more:

> "Now my soul is troubled. And what should I say—
> 'Father, save me from this hour'? But it was for this that I
> came to this hour. Father, glorify your name." Then a voice
> sounded from heaven: "I have glorified it, and I will glorify
> it again." Some of the crowd who were there and heard
> said that it was thunder; others said, "An angel spoke to
> him." But Jesus replied to them, "It was not for my sake but
> for yours that this voice sounded." (John 12:27–30)

At these crucial junctures in Jesus' career, God not only stands with Jesus in his work but provides verbal confirmation of Jesus' mission.[11]

However much these instances of divine speaking may appear to confirm Jesus' confessional stance, however, they seem finally and catastrophically overwhelmed by divine silence. For when Jesus goes to Jerusalem for the final time and is arrested, tried, and executed as a criminal, no heavenly voice speaks in protest. This silence of God becomes palpable in Gethsemane, when Jesus' struggle with the destiny that lies before him is depicted as taking place in isolation both from the weary disciples and from the God who is addressed but does not answer (Matt. 26:36–46). Nor is it possible to view Jesus' loneliness in the garden as a matter of testing, in which God's absence is only apparent. Such explanations are shattered by the brutal fact of the crucifixion, which Jesus himself interprets as evidence of his having been abandoned by God (Matt. 27:46; Mark 15:33).

If the validity of Jesus' claims rest on the witness of the Father, this witness's silence on Good Friday seems to demand the conclusion that Jesus has been rejected by God (Gal 3:13). From this point of view, even the taunting of the crowds who look on at the crucifixion appears theologically justified: it only stands to reason that if Jesus were God's Son, God would not let him die in agony (Matt. 27:39–44 and pars.). Indeed, even Jesus' own disciples seem to have interpreted events in this way initially (Luke 24:19–21). Yet it soon came to be their experience that the cross was not the end of Jesus' story. Out of the silence of Calvary had come an act of power in which God raised Jesus from the dead (Acts 2:32; 4:10; 13:30; 1 Cor. 15:4) and bestowed upon him "all authority on heaven and earth" (Matt. 28:18; compare Phil. 2:9–11).

God's silence in the face of the crucifixion remains an inexpungeable fact.[12] Yet when viewed in terms of the whole of Jesus' ministry, God's silence on Good Friday discloses the link between the God Jesus proclaims and the social location from which this proclamation is made. If Jesus' solidarity with the marginalized constitutes the core of his claim about where and how God is present in the world, his death on the cross puts this claim to the test. For the ultimate seriousness of God's commitment to build God's realm "from the outside in" is decided by the extent to which Jesus, precisely as the "beloved Son" whose ministry inaugurates this realm, not only works among the marginalized, but allows himself to be pushed to the margins.[13]

In this context, God's absence from Calvary should not be understood to mean that the one Jesus calls Father is essentially unaffected by what happens there. Quite the contrary, if Jesus is truly the bearer of God's realm, then the death of Jesus would appear to indicate both the defeat of that realm and the impotence of the God in whose name it is proclaimed. To the extent that the rule of God is established through Jesus' ministry, the fate of the Father must be regarded as inseparable from that of the Son. It follows, as Jürgen Moltmann points out, that the death of Jesus threatens God's own being, as constituted by the mutual confession of the Father and the Son, with dissolution:

> The Father forsakes the Son "for us"—that is to say, in order
> to become God and Father of the forsaken. The Father
> "delivers up" the Son in order through him to become the
> Father of those who have been delivered up. . . . The Son
> suffers death in this forsakenness. The Father suffers the
> death of the Son. And when in the descent to hell the Son
> loses the Father, then in this judgment the Father also loses
> the Son. Here the innermost life of the Trinity is at stake.
> Here the communicating life of the Father turns into infi-
> nite pain over the sacrifice of the Son. Here the responding
> love of the Son becomes infinite suffering over his repulsion
> and rejection by the Father. What happens on Golgotha
> reaches into the innermost depths of the Godhead, putting
> its impress on the trinitarian life in eternity.[14]

The God who claims Jesus as the beloved Son has bound divine identity—and thus divine destiny—to the fate of this human being. Consequently, in Jesus' death, God has everything to lose: because it is Jesus who in his confession manifests the Father's rule, and because a dead Jesus is no longer capable of confession, the conclusion follows that in Jesus' death the Father's life, too, must come to an end.

To take Jesus' death seriously is therefore to recognize that on the cross, the relationship between Jesus and the one he calls Father is not simply stretched to the breaking point; it actually breaks. It breaks because death is the end of even the possibility of relation-ship (Pss. 6:4–5; 28:1; 30:9; 88:3–5, 10–12; 143:7; Isa. 38:18–19). Because the identity of the Father and the Son is defined by their relationship of mutual confession, theological talk of the "death of

God" should not be restricted to the physical death of Jesus (though Jesus' death is its defining moment), but should rather be understood to refer to the sundering of the confessional relationship that constitutes the life of the Father and the Son alike. At the same time, however, it should be recognized that this sundering actually serves to confirm God's commitment to live and reign from the margins. To have answered Jesus on the cross would have been for God to pull back from the margins and thus to have held God's own identity as the Father of the Son dearer than the fate of those who have both preceded and followed Jesus to the cross (see Matt. 26:53).

That God did not draw back, but rather "so loved the world as to give the only-begotten Son" (John 3:16), means that nothing—not even God's own identity as the Father of the Son—stands in the way of God's solidarity with the least of this world. The divine silence at the cross thus becomes, paradoxically, a sign of God's presence there in the person of Jesus: God is truly present with us in Jesus only if it is in the crucified Jesus alone that God is present on Calvary.[15]

Only in this way does faith in God's presence amid all the other instances of death and abandonment in history acquire any degree of plausibility; otherwise it is merely a pious projection. For this presence in the mode of absence is not simply a clever paradox, it is the final test of God's presence with us in Jesus of Nazareth. If up to that point it is God's voice that declares Jesus the beloved Son, now it is the very silence of God that allows a human being to say, "Truly this . . . was the Son of God" (Mark 15:39).

THE CONFESSION OF THE HOLY SPIRIT

Notwithstanding the significance of the centurion's witness, it is only in light of Easter morning that the Father's silence before the cross can be counted as evidence of God's full presence there in Jesus. And yet nothing could be a more mistaken in this context than to view Easter as a simple reversal of Good Friday, through which Jesus returns to his earthly existence.[16] That the risen Jesus continues to bear the marks of his passion (John 20:27) shows that the fact of his death remains an indelible part of his history. The good news of Easter is precisely that death, which had seemed to define the end of Jesus' history, is now past and thus a part of his history. The Easter miracle is not that Jesus has cheated death (in which case, the suspicion would remain that death might still be a part of his future), but that Jesus has been raised from the dead, so that death is for him ever after something that is behind him (see Rom. 6:9).

Because both the fact and the circumstances of Jesus' death remain an inexpungeable part of his history, his resurrection cannot simply be interpreted as a change of heart on the part of the Father. If the scandal of the cross—and with it the seriousness of God's commitment to communion with humankind—are to be preserved, it is necessary for Christian reflection to take seriously the fact that on Calvary the relationship between the Father and the Son was broken. To the extent that this relationship is constitutive of the being of the Father and Son alike, this breach cannot have been healed by the action of either person without the tacit admission that it was, in the final analysis, illusory.

If Jesus were the agent of his own resurrection, one would be forced to conclude that he had not really died; similarly, if the work of resurrection is attributed to the Father, then it follows that God's abandonment of the Son on Calvary was less than complete. The biblical summary formula "God raised Jesus from the dead" (Acts 3:15; 4:10; 13:30; Rom. 10:9; Gal. 1:1; 1 Pet. 1:21) notwithstanding, the resurrection cannot be attributed to the Father or the Son.

In this context, it is important to listen to the biblical claim that Jesus "was confirmed as Son of God with power according to the Spirit of holiness in his resurrection from the dead" (Rom. 1:4). Only God can vindicate Jesus' identity as the beloved Son; but the separation of the Father from the Son cannot be overcome from within—by the Father's intervening to rescue Jesus, or by Jesus not really dying—without casting doubt on the reality of that separation. It is in this context that the Holy Spirit is designated by Scripture as the one who bears witness that the love that unites the Father and the Son is stronger than death.[17] If the confession of the Son by the Father and the Father by the Son finds its limit on Calvary, in the resurrection the Spirit bears witness that even this limit is no limit, so that in the Spirit the mutual confession of the Father and the Son is preserved through death.

As the witness to the power of the love of the Father and the Son to endure even death, the Spirit functions as the ultimate guarantor both of divine identity and of divine unity. But the Spirit is not, for that reason, a God other or higher than the Father or the Son. On the contrary, Scripture clearly states that the Spirit is sent by the Father for the sole purpose of bearing witness to Jesus as the Son of the Father (John 14:26). In this way, the Spirit seems to function as a sort of advance guard for the mission of the Son. Thus, it is the Spirit who is operative at the incarnation (Matt. 1:20; Luke 1:35), who comes upon Jesus at his baptism (Matt. 1:16 and pars.), and who drives him into the wilderness to be tempted (Matt. 4:1 and pars.). It is also the Spirit whose power Jesus claims for his deeds (Matt. 12:28), and who he promises will come to lead the disciples into "all truth" after the crucifixion (John 16:13). And at the crucifixion, when Jesus "commends [his] spirit" to the Father (Luke 24:46) and "hands over" the Spirit (John 19:30), the Spirit goes on ahead again, meeting Jesus on the far side of death and raising him from it (1 Pet. 3:18–19).

Therefore, if Jesus speaks together with the Father, this does not take place without the Spirit speaking together with Jesus. Indeed, if the mission of Jesus, as the beloved Son, is to confess the Father even unto death, it is the Spirit's mission to confess Jesus as the Son even beyond death, so that the Spirit's work functions as the necessary context for the mutual confession of the Father and the Son both before and after Good Friday.

The fact of being so completely oriented to the other two persons can make the Spirit seem impersonal, but nothing could be further from the truth. As Catherine LaCugna and Wolfhart Pannenberg have both argued, the measure of personhood in the divine life is not self-sufficiency, but orientation to the other.[18] The personhood of the Son lies in obedience to the Father's will; the personhood of the Father lies in handing over the realm of God to the Son. Against this background, the Spirit might be viewed as the most "personal" of all, as that hypostasis whose personhood consists entirely in bearing witness to the mutual love of the Father and the Son.

TRINITARIAN LIFE AS THE GROUND OF
CHRISTIAN CONFESSION

It is in terms of this mutual confession of the three persons that the place of human confession must be understood. Christians confess that there is one God—the same God Jesus Christ called Father. But because they cannot talk about this God without also talking of Jesus Christ, they find it necessary to confess God the Son in order clearly to confess God the Father. And because, in light of the catastrophe of Good Friday and the exultation of Easter morning, they finally cannot talk about the Father or the Son without also talking about the Holy Spirit; they find themselves confessing God in three persons, Father, Son, and Holy Spirit.

This threefold confession is not to be understood simply as a peculiarity of human language, as if we were forced to confess God under three names because of some inherent limit in our ability to perceive a deeper unity. Rather, the triune form of Christian confession reflects the fact that God's own being is constituted by the pattern of confession by which the three persons are related, in which no one of the three lives apart from the other two. The Father lives as the one who is confessed by the Son in the Spirit; the Son exists as the one who is confessed by the Spirit of the Father; the Spirit exists as the one who confesses Jesus as the Son of the Father. It is therefore not merely we as human beings who are unable to speak of the Father without also mentioning the Son and Spirit; the Father also is unable to do so: begetting the Son and breathing forth the Spirit is precisely how—or, rather, *who*—the Father is. Similarly, the Son and the Spirit *are* through their distinctive ways of confessing the Father as the one God who will some day be all in all.[19]

In this way, the ecclesial act of confession is grounded in the structure of the divine life itself. If confession, as the act of speaking with others, is the way in which we encounter God, it is because the act of speaking together with another is the way in which God *is* in God's own self. Confession is, therefore, more than a window on the divine life; it is the act of conforming oneself to that life. This commitment takes historically particular form for God and human beings alike through the person Jesus of

Nazareth. For Jesus' confession of the Father does not simply point Christians to God, it is actually constitutive of God's being. That Christians address God as Father through the Son and in the Spirit therefore reflects that God lives as the Father only through the Son and in the Spirit. This life is actualized in a mutual confession of the three persons, the content of which is both fully defined and vindicated in Jesus' resurrection from the dead.

THE SPIRIT'S BREAKING OPEN OF THE DIVINE LIFE

It may seem strange to describe the resurrection as an act of confession. What happens on Easter seems more naturally conceived in nonverbal terms than as an act of speaking together with another, in spite of the fact that none of the canonical Gospels contains a description of the resurrection. To single out confession as the mode by which the divine life is actualized seems comprehensible in terms of the relationship between the Father and the Son: Jesus' confession of the Father's reign among the poor is, after all, the basic theme of his earthly ministry; similarly, Scripture offers examples of the verbal confession of the Son by the Father, albeit on a far more limited scale. By contrast, confessional activity on the part of the Spirit would seem much harder to pin down.

And yet the Holy Spirit is not just one character among others within the biblical narrative. In contrast to Mary or Jesus—or even the one called Father—the Spirit seems disturbingly anonymous, a formless power that "blows where it wishes"—and yet of this same Spirit it is said that "you hear its voice" (John 3:8). The question is where we hear it. For the Spirit does not speak directly from heaven; neither does it become incarnate in the manner of the Son. Indeed, the Spirit's life is defined and determined entirely by its witness to Jesus as the one in and through whom God has realized the divine will to live in solidarity with a fallen creation. This will reaches its climax on Calvary, when even death is shown not to represent a limit to this solidarity and thus becomes incorporated into the relationship of Father and Son that defines the divine life itself.

Because of this acceptance of death, Jesus remains the center of Christian confession of the triune God, who lives and works from the margins. If the Spirit authenticates this life in the resurrection, it is not because the Spirit moves even farther to the margins than Jesus did but because the Spirit bears witness to Jesus as the very presence of God at the margins. So close is this connection that according to Scripture, a spirit may be recognized as the Holy Spirit of God precisely by its confession of Jesus come in the flesh (1 John 4:2; compare 1 Cor. 12:3).

And yet the Spirit does not speak in its own right. The Spirit points away from itself to Jesus through the confession of human beings. This process begins with Jesus himself, who, having been raised in the power of the Spirit, testifies to that fact to his doubting disciples (Matt. 28:16–17; Luke 24:31–34; John 20:19–20; 26–27).[20] Insofar as the risen Jesus promises to give the Spirit to his disciples as the basis for their own testimony to the world at large (Acts 1:8; John 14:26; compare Luke 24:49; Matt. 10:19–20 and pars.), he confirms the inseparability of the Spirit's witness from the active participation of human beings. Moreover, this human mediation of the Spirit's witness is further evidence of the divine commitment to the marginalized.

As already noted, if the resurrection had happened other than by the mediation of the Spirit—if, for example, Jesus' death simply had been reversed by the Father—then God's commitment to humankind would have to be interpreted quite differently. While human nature would have been redeemed through Jesus, this redemption would have taken place at the expense of the whole of humanity, Jew and Gentile, who share the guilt of having condemned Jesus to the cross. That is, even though God's good creation were vindicated through the redemption of the righteous human being Jesus of Nazareth, this sort of victory would have to be characterized as brutal and tyrannical.[21] God would remain above death, and thus above real solidarity with the fate of a fallen humankind: human communion with God in Jesus would remain real but profoundly unfree.

But Jesus was not raised in this way. Instead, Jesus was raised in the power of the Spirit, in a way that vindicates God's solidarity with those same human beings who had left Jesus to die on the cross, even to the extent of including those same sinful people in this vindication. In brief, God establishes communion with human beings only in such a way as to allow human beings to establish communion with God. This reciprocity between God and humankind, in which God's own deity as Father and Son is confirmed through the witness of the church in the power of the Spirit, thereby represents the culminating example of God's working from the margins. In the work of the Spirit, God's divinity is confirmed as one in which communion, both inside and outside the divine life, is based on a respect for the other in its otherness. The Father's love for the created order is based on a respect for the integrity of that order that has its roots in the Father's respect for the integrity of the Son within the Godhead.[22]

In the incarnation, God binds the divine destiny to the human in a way that extends to death itself. This solidarity begins as a ministry among the marginalized, those excluded from full participation in and acceptance by the covenant community, signaling that God is present precisely among such persons, building the covenant community from the outside in rather than the top down. It extends to the marginalization of this God's own self in the trial and execution of Jesus. The crucifixion thus represents a crisis in the divine life. On the one hand, the distance between the Father in heaven and the Son on earth becomes an absolute separation, in which the curse of God falls upon the crucified Jesus. On the other hand, it is also precisely at this point that the presence of God in Christ is confirmed.

All of which is only to repeat the point that the Christian God is to be found only in history, and in history only among the marginalized, and among the marginalized as the Jew Jesus of Nazareth. But that is only the first part of God's will to vindicate the goodness of human creation. The character of this vindication remains unclear apart from the confession of the decisive unity of the Father and the Son given by the Spirit in the resurrection. As the one who bears witness to the Jesus who lived and died at the margins, the Spirit is also active at the margins. For while the Spirit's witness, as that which vindicates God's unique and definitive presence in Jesus of Nazareth, is for this reason rightly regarded as God's own, it does not appear directly as such. Instead, the Spirit's witness—that witness upon which the divine life itself depends—is mediated through human life, in the confession of those who in the Spirit are enabled to confess that Jesus is God.

It is therefore through the Holy Spirit that God's commitment to the margins is fulfilled, since in the Spirit God's own life, constituted in the mutual love of the Father and the Son in the Spirit, is realized in community with human life. In other words, the life that is revealed as triune is one that refuses to be apart from free communion with that which is not divine (Rev. 21:3) and, indeed, apart from those who have chosen to oppose the divine (Rom. 5:8). This is not to suggest that God is somehow incomplete prior to the resurrection. For it is precisely *as* the triune reality of Father, Son, and Holy Spirit, acting out of free love for that which is not divine, that God wills to create and redeem at all.

To suppose otherwise would only cast doubt on the claim to divinity of the one who confronts us through the ministry of Jesus of Nazareth. And yet while the logic of belief demands that we confess God as three-in-one from all eternity, this position does not preclude the idea that, as the Trinity we know through Jesus Christ (which is to say, as the one who has bound the divine destiny to that of human beings), God's life is fulfilled in the work of redemption.[23] To hesitate at this point would be to mistake divine freedom (which properly refers to the fact that God has willed to be none other than the Father of Jesus Christ) for divine caprice (which, if taken seriously, would leave open the possibility that the promise of salvation in Jesus Christ was perhaps not God's final word to us). By bearing witness in Christ and the church that God refuses to live apart from a redeemed creation, God the Spirit reveals a God who has put the divine life at stake for—and is therefore affected by—that which is not God.

All of which merely reaffirms the idea that the Spirit's role within the Godhead is inseparable from its place in the economy of salvation: in confirming the being of God, the Spirit also confirms that which is not God in its relationship to God. It is thus by virtue of the Spirit, according to Paul, that human beings are able to call God "Abba" (Rom. 8:9). In so doing, the Spirit neither equates human beings with God nor reduces them to nothing before God; rather, the Spirit establishes human beings precisely as such—as sons and daughters in the Son rather than beings willing their own dissolution as creatures in the misguided desire to be "like God" (Gen. 3).[24]

This process begins in the divine life itself, as the work of the Spirit in the resurrection establishes the integrity of the Father and the Son over against the threat of dissolution. It is extended to humankind in and through that relationship, so that the divine way of guaranteeing the particularity of the trinitarian persons spills over to include and encompass the integrity of the created order in general and of human beings as free subjects in particular (see 1 Cor. 2:9–13).[25]

Indeed, the working of the Spirit in and through humanity is not only the consequence of Jesus' ministry but also its precondition. As at the resurrection, so throughout the history of Israel and in Jesus' own life, the Spirit goes ahead of God as the advance guard of the divine will. In the history of Israel that functions as the immediate historical context for Jesus' appearing, the Spirit guides and shapes the community by speaking through the prophets. This sending of the Spirit is understood to be a foretaste of the expected realm of God, in which the Spirit is to be poured out on all Israel (Joel 2:28–29; compare Acts 2:17–18).

In none of these cases, however, does the Spirit cease to be the Spirit of Jesus Christ. Indeed, it has been a persistent theme of Christian interpretation of Scripture that the Spirit's identity is inseparable from its witness to Jesus, no less before than after Christmas. The evangelists in particular view the prophets as those chosen vessels through whom the Spirit foretold Christ's coming in the flesh, and treat Jesus' ministry as in some measure authenticated by this prior witness.[26]

In this way, the mediate character of the Spirit's witness is evident already in the Old Testament, as God's will to be with human beings takes the form of a divine empowering of individuals to stand and speak with God. Still, this witness remains anticipatory and indirect: the prophets look forward to what cannot yet be seen or heard (Matt. 13:17). Only with the incarnation is it truly possible to confess the God of Israel in the literal sense, because only with the incarnation is God physically present in a person, who is Jesus Christ.

Specifically Christian confession consists precisely in taking this physicality seriously, recognizing that true confession is time- and space-specific. As the would-be disciples who confront Jesus on the road discover, to confess Jesus is to share his precarious existence among the marginalized, cut off from society's efforts to protect itself from the contingencies of existence in time and space (Luke 9:57–62; Matt. 8:19–22).

TRINITY AS GOD FROM THE OUTSIDE IN

The burden of chapters 3–5 was to establish that the biblical God builds the covenant community from the outside in. This metaphor is based on the recognition that the community of Israel, like every other community, can be characterized in terms of a center of leadership, which functions to preserve and transmit the communal identity and which serves as the fundamental measure of status within the community. The margins are constituted by those who stand farthest from the center while still being counted and counting themselves as part of the community.

Still, by virtue of their distance from the center, the marginalized tend not to be viewed as constitutive of the identity of the community of which they are a part. Often they are simply ignored. At other times, their social location leads those at the center to call into question not only their loyalty to the community but even their status as members of it.

That the God of Israel should make covenant with a community of slaves and, having established it, continue to shape it by acting through more or less marginal members therefore constitutes a significant reversal of sociological convention. This reversal reaches its climax in Jesus' proclamation that God's rule breaks into history at (and even beyond) the margins of the covenant community. And yet so long as God's own self is understood as fundamentally distinct from this process, as an immovable center whose appearance at the margins is little more than a sociological side effect of human sin, the margins and those who occupy them lack decisive theological significance.

From this more traditional perspective, the theologian's task is one of attempting to discern the timeless reality of God beyond the accidental sociological features of divine activity in history. This temptation to try to abstract some fixed content of the gospel from the sociohistorical conditions of its proclamation can seem altogether natural, when a fuller trinitarian perspective is obscured by exclusive concentration on the teaching of Jesus as the final, definitive revelation of God's will for humankind.

This temptation need not take the form of an explicit ecclesiastical triumphalism, for it is rooted less in an exaggerated estimation of human abilities than in an insufficiently developed doctrine of God. Even Karl Barth, who takes great pains to distinguish the church's authority from God's, seems in the final analysis to understand both forms of authority as binding decrees that render further conversation superfluous:

> Because and to the extent that it rests on an insight given to the Church, a genuine confession can and must speak authoritatively: it cannot simply publish its findings as a subject for discussion and free choice. What the confession formulates and proclaims claims to be Church dogma. In saying Credo it has characterized its pronouncements as those whose content it cannot and will not force on anyone, but with which it challenges everyone to take up a position.[27]

The last sentence is particularly important in the present context. For while Barth's rejection of the use of force must be taken seriously, liberation theologians would doubtless point out that it is one thing to exclude the use of force in principle and another to give teeth to this principle in light of the sociological realities of communal life. On the basis of his conclusions regarding the absolute priority of God's Word, however, Barth argues that the abuse of ecclesiastical authority or freedom (that is, authority or freedom exercised apart from submission to the Word) is just not a genuine possibility for the church: "We do not, therefore, need a subsequent safeguard against the possibility that 'freedom in the Church' will become dangerous and develop into a freedom in opposition to the Word, an emancipation from the Word. This possibility is excluded from the outset and by the nature of the case."[28]

Barth is not blind to the fact that such abuse does arise; his point is simply that it is indefensible on the basis of the internal logic of the Word of God and therefore cannot be prevented by the addition of some further ecclesiological safeguard (like solidarity with the marginalized) which would be any less subject to abuse. Granted that no provision will be likely to eliminate ecclesiastical abuse of authority, however, the question is the way in which a given approach to theology views the relationship between debate and decision in the life of the church. In this context, Barth's approach seems to tilt the scales against the critique of an established church practice. For all his emphasis on the sovereignty of the Word and the importance of debate, Barth's focus remains the goal of the process, when the church's teaching is given definitive form and debate comes to an end. To be sure, Barth does not regard any (written) confessional position, however well established, as irreformable; but his stress on the fact that the Word as confessed in the church is not to be treated merely "as a subject for discussion" does raise questions over the degree to which the life of the church under the Word can indeed be characterized as a "debate."

To question Barth on this point is not to deny that debate must come to an end if the church is to have a clear position on matters of faith and practice, still less to suggest that solidarity with the marginalized is by itself a guarantee of doctrinal correctness. As noted in the previous chapter, the margins are not the source of the gospel; that distinction belongs solely to Jesus Christ. The margins are, however, the necessary context for any preaching being vindicated *as* gospel, so that all talk of gospel is theologically vacuous apart from active encounter with the margins. Nor does this conclusion relativize Jesus' significance. On the contrary, it is rooted precisely in Christian faith in the ultimate significance of Jesus

Christ who, as a person whose historical particularity acquires universal significance through his resurrection from the dead, cannot be separated from the concrete circumstances of his appearing.

It is from this point that attention to the particularity of Jesus undergirds trinitarian doctrine. Because they regard the presence and power of God's rule as truly inseparable from Jesus, Christians affirm that Jesus is God. But the fact that this same Jesus also differentiates himself from the God of Israel points to a tension within the divine life, in which the one to whom God has entrusted the ministry of God's realm seems over the course of Jesus' ministry to stand at an ever greater distance from the God he calls Father, culminating in his apparent abandonment by this God on the cross. And yet nothing could be more mistaken than to view this conclusion as substantiating a fundamental break between God and the margins. On the contrary, in light of the resurrection, it is possible to see that the silence on Golgotha is actually part and parcel of a larger divine solidarity with the margins implicit in Jesus' message. For the Father to have saved the Son from the cross would have amounted to a drawing back from (and thus a falsification of) that divine solidarity with humankind at the heart of Jesus' preaching. To be sure, God's absence on Good Friday does mean that the mutual confession of the Father and the Son comes to an end on Calvary—but that very fact is consistent with the proposition that in and through Jesus, God shares human life even to the point of death.

Admittedly, it is only in light of the resurrection that this interpretation is possible, but this fact does not in any way negate the constitutive significance of Jesus' earthly ministry for defining the divine identity. Quite the contrary, the fact that it is precisely Jesus of Nazareth who is proclaimed as risen means the vindication of the earthly Jesus—with all his social and religious peculiarities—as the only-begotten Son. At the same time, the breach between the Father and the Son experienced on Good Friday points to the role of the Holy Spirit as the divine agent of the resurrection.

On one hand, this Spirit is to be recognized as truly God because only in light of the Spirit's work is it possible to confess the divinity of the Father and the Son; on the other, the Spirit cannot be thought of as God over against the Father and the Son, since the

Spirit's identity is constituted entirely by the act of confessing the mutual love of the other two persons. Yet this confession, far from being localized in some isolated divine sphere, actually sets the capstone to divine solidarity with the marginalized insofar as it is mediated through human beings who, precisely by virtue of the crucified Jesus' solidarity with them, are revealed to stand at the farthest remove from divine reality and, through Jesus, thereby to be incorporated in it.

In this way, the confessional nature of the church's authority is rooted in the structure of God's own life, which—as realized through the life, death, and resurrection of Jesus Christ in the power of the Spirit—involves the church. Humankind is not led to participate in the divine life passively or against its will but through a process of confession in the Spirit that both reflects and completes the intra-trinitarian relationship between the Father and the Son. In the church as in the Godhead, the work of confession is structured in terms of a relationship between center and margins. Moreover, this relationship has a definite order: just as the Father is the reference point for the Son's ministry, so the traditions defined and transmitted by the communal leadership serve as the reference point for the work of proclaiming the gospel.

As Athanasius and later the Cappadocians argued strenuously, however, the presence of this internal ordering of ministries should in no way be understood to imply that the Father is either superior to or independent of the other persons, as though it were possible to speak of the Father apart from the Son. On the contrary, it was their contention that the very act of speaking of God as Father involved an inescapable reference to the Son, who for this reason was regarded as constitutive of the Godhead—and therefore of the Father's identity *as* Father. Similarly, to concede a role to the ecclesiastical center as the source of the gospel's verbal components provides no grounds for separating the center from the margins, as though the gospel possessed some "absolute" content that could either be defined or defended independently of the circumstances of its proclamation. The model of confession means rather that both Christian identity and the authority that goes with it are inseparable from social commitment to the marginalized.

That this commitment must be social and not merely intellectual or verbal follows from the fact that God's Word did not remain suspended in the heavens but "became flesh and dwelt among us." The incarnation constitutes a fundamental act of confession on God's part that also makes it possible to understand God's own life as one of confession. This confession is the subject of the New Testament, the narrative form of which supports the contention that both the identity of this person in whom God was present and the substance of his message are alike inseparable from the physical conditions of his earthly existence. But if the confession of Jesus cannot be separated from the margins, neither can that of Christians who presume to speak in his name. Therefore, the fact that God appears (and that Christians are therefore called to live) at the margins should not be viewed as an arbitrary decree of the divine will, but bound up with the structure of God's own life. Life at the margins is not subsequent (let alone incidental) to the act of proclaiming the gospel; it is constitutive of any instance of a proclamation's being gospel in the first place. Christians can speak with God only because God speaks with them; and the content of this speaking, as derived from its divine source, cannot be separated from (because it is partly a product of) the context in which it is spoken.

The demand that the church live at the margins, therefore, has nothing to do with the church's questioning its own authority. It is rather a corollary of the church's right to claim the authority of the God of Jesus Christ, whose identity and authority are constituted at the margins. The Christian doctrine of the Trinity is simply a summary account of this recognition that the divine life, as the mutual confession of the Father and the Son in the power of the Spirit, is lived from the outside in.

chapter seven

AUTHORITY AND THE POWER OF NAMING

This book took as its starting point the erosion of the prestige once enjoyed by the Christian churches in Western society. As the ways in which the churches' teachings have been used as an ideological lever to silence competing accounts of reality have become more widely recognized, Christians have been challenged from a number of quarters to defend their claim to teach with authority.

Often this challenge has been understood by Christians and non-Christians alike in zero-sum terms, meaning that any concession of public accountability on the part of the church is assumed to imply a proportional diminution of its claim to teach with authority. This way of viewing the matter presupposes that possession of authority entails immunity from criticism. Ultimate authority is conceived as something fixed above and beyond the contingencies of history, and which therefore provides an anchor for human thought and action that is unaffected by what happens within time and space.

CLAIMING AUTHORITY TO NAME GOD

Within the field of theology, this zero-sum framework means that every bit of authority attributed to God comes at the expense of human beings, and vice versa. Wherever God is active, human beings must be passive, and wherever humanity is active, God must withdraw from the scene: when one side gains, the other loses.

Given this framework, it is invariable that one or the other party will ultimately seem superfluous. Where (as in much of modern Western culture since the Enlightenment) a premium is placed on human authority and responsibility, God becomes an unnecessary hypothesis.

Alternatively, where God is valued, humankind seems by necessity to be reduced to a puppetlike existence, totally subject to the whims of an all-powerful deity. In this way, Christians seemed forced to choose between two equally troublesome positions: if we are indeed "persons under authority" (Matt. 8:9), then there is no place for individual responsibility (as the Nuremberg defendants claimed); but if we are responsible, then it is an act of bad faith to appeal to some higher, divine authority to justify our actions (as Marxists and existentialists maintain).

It has been the burden of the preceding pages to show that this model of authority is fundamentally inconsistent with the biblical understanding of the relationship between God and humanity. According to the Gospels, the highest authority is not exercised from the top down but "from the outside in," as God's sovereignty is established from a position of the deepest possible commitment to and solidarity with those who, to all appearances, have the least claim to authority.

This model of authority implies an ongoing process of questioning established practices within the community of faith. If God rules from the margins, then it stands to reason that the church will only be able to hear God's Word as the good news it is intended to be to the extent that it looks for God on its margins and thereby subverts the sociological tendency for authority to gravitate toward the community's established centers of leadership.

Not that this commitment to the margins implies a disparagement of the center and the traditions collected there, as though the content of God's Word could be defined by simple opposition to established teaching and equated directly with the words of the marginalized. Because Jesus remains the Sovereign of the church and its gospel, no party in the church can be presumed to have a monopoly on the gospel simply by virtue of its ecclesial location. But because the church's Sovereign is Jesus, Christians will only be fooling themselves if they suppose that the gospel can be proclaimed faithfully without regard to the response of the marginalized. The gospel is, after all, good news for the poor; it follows that if the poor fail to hear the church's proclamation as good news, the evangelical character of that proclamation is open to serious question.

The practical implications of this point emerge already with the seemingly elementary task of naming God. If God's own destiny is inseparable from the fate of the marginalized, then it is impossible to suppose that this God can be accurately named apart from reference to their experience. In this context, feminist theologians in particular have pointed out that there is a striking contradiction between the commitment to the marginalized characteristic of the God Jesus calls Father and the way in which the churches' practice of naming this God as "Father" has served to exclude women from full participation in the community of faith.

To be sure, theologians since the time of Athanasius have insisted that the use of the terms "Father" and "Son" should not be taken to imply that the divine persons have male gender; nevertheless, the prominence of these terms in the liturgy has done nothing to challenge the churches' reliance on exclusively masculine imagery for God.[1] Nor has the principle that God is beyond gender prevented male theologians up to the present day from appealing to Jesus' maleness as grounds for affirming that men alone are properly suited for positions of ecclesiastical leadership. Finally (and, perhaps, most profoundly), feminists have argued that the exclusive use of father-son language for God defines the central symbol of the Christian faith in hierarchical terms, with the result that all reality interpreted by this faith comes to be viewed according to an essentially dualistic scheme of upper and lower, super- and subordinate.[2]

The force of these and related charges has not prevented feminist theologians from arguing that such developments constitute a betrayal of Jesus' own practice of subverting established social hierarchies. Often it is noted that Jesus' use of father-son language could actually function to destabilize patriarchy within his own first-century Palestinian context. Sandra Schneiders puts it this way:

In Jesus' culture the father-son metaphor was the only one capable of carrying the meaning of his integral involvement in the work of salvation originated by God. Second, by his use of "Abba" for God and his presentation of God as the father of the prodigal, Jesus was able to transform totally the patriarchal God-image. He healed the father metaphor which had been patriarchalized in the image of human power structures and restored it to the original meaning of divine origination in and through love. Third, he delegitimized human patriarchy by invalidating its appeal to divine institution.[3]

This kind of attention to Jesus' cultural location is certainly important if his ability to be the bearer of good news to women as well as men is not to be dismissed out of hand as incompatible with his particularity as a male human being. At the same time, however, it may be asked whether appeal to Jesus' practice is sufficient to meet feminists' more fundamental concerns. If (as liberation theologians of both sexes would claim) the liberating character of Jesus' ministry hinges on the claim that in him God identifies with the marginalized, then the fact of Jesus' maleness might seem to mark a limit to divine self-marginalization that would leave women outside the bounds of God's saving presence.

In response to this concern, Elizabeth Johnson has made the provocative suggestion that Jesus' maleness, far from compromising the integrity of his message, provides the key to appreciating its radical character: "If in a patriarchal culture a woman had preached compassionate love and enacted a style of authority that serves, she would most certainly have been greeted with a colossal shrug. Is this not what women are supposed to do by nature? But from a social position of male privilege Jesus preached and acted in this way, and herein lies the summons."[4] Seen from this perspective, Jesus' ministry entails a subversion not of Jesus' male particularity as such, but of the supposition that gender difference implies the subordination of one gender to another. It is precisely by virtue of the fact that he, as a man, assumes the condition of the marginalized and thereby lives out a model of authority as service that Jesus effects the subversion of social relationships of super- and subordination that Rosemary Radford Ruether describes as the "kenosis of patriarchy."[5]

Even if it is granted that Jesus himself subverts the patriarchal conventions of his society, however, does not his self-defined relationship of absolute obedience to the one he calls Father (see, for example, Matt. 26:42 and pars.; John 5:30; 6:38; Phil. 2:8; Heb. 5:7–8) reinscribe them on an even more fundamental level? Certainly history shows how easily the model of Jesus' submission to an omnipotent Father-God can come to be viewed not only as the prescribed attitude for human beings in general before God, but also, more specifically, as normative for women in their relations with men.[6] In this way, the metaphorical framework established by the use of father-son language for speaking of the relationship between Jesus and God can serve as more or less explicit justification for all manner of physical and psychological abuse of society's most vulnerable by those who hold the reins of power.[7]

It is in this context that it is vital to insist on the mutuality of the relation between Jesus and the God he calls Father. Because God's identity as Father is established only in Jesus' act of confession as the Son, the consequences of Jesus' death are no less serious for the First Person than for the Second. This is not to deny that the relationship between the Father and the Son entails a certain order. The biblical witness distinguishes a number of times between the Father as the one who sends and the Son who is sent (see, for example, Matt. 10:40 and pars.; John 5:23–24,37; 17:3, 8, 20–23; 20:21); moreover, this order provides an important basis for distinguishing between the two persons.

But within the narrative framework of the Gospels, the presence of order does not imply a hierarchy in which either person is subordinate to the other.[8] After all, the act of sending the Son, far from entailing the subordination of the Second Person to the First, is understood biblically as the act by which the Father entrusts the divine rule—and thus the divine life itself—to the incarnate Son (John 3:35; 1 Cor. 15:27).[9] If it is from this God that all creaturely fatherhood is named (Eph. 3:15), then it would seem to follow that true fatherhood entails entrusting one's destiny to those (especially women and children) who are of least account within the patriarchal order—a practical sign of which evidently includes refusing to claim titles like "father" in the first place (Matt. 23:9; compare 18:1–5; 20:25–28 and pars.).[10]

This last point brings us directly to the question of the language Christians use to talk about God. There is no getting around the fact that the terms "Father" and "Son" are frequent and inexpungeable features of New Testament language for God. Christians would be dishonest if they attempted to sidestep this fact. Moreover, as noted above, these terms have a subversive function within the Gospel texts with respect to their patriarchal background. But it would be equally dishonest for Christians to downplay the ways in which the use of these terms serves, intentionally or not, to obscure or even subvert the good news of Jesus Christ for women.

In this context, the most important point to be made is that the God whom Jesus names as Father is in that very act revealed as one whose identity consists in allowing the divine self to be named by another. To be sure, this act of naming is not arbitrary; and because the God Christians confess is none other than the one Jesus called Father, it is hard to see how it would be possible to identify this God apart from a living memory of the story of Jesus and his own practice of divine naming. At the same time, however, other ways of naming this God could be ruled out only if the divine identity were exhausted by the relationship of Father and Son proclaimed by Jesus. As argued in the previous chapter, however, this is emphatically not the case.

Although the resurrection is the event through which God's identity as Father and Son is vindicated, it is also the occasion for Christian reflection on the Third Person of the Trinity, God the Holy Spirit. Christian experience of the Spirit suggests that the work of resurrection cannot be attributed either to the Father or to the Son without compromising the fullness of divine solidarity with humankind manifest in Jesus' death on the cross. In the face of the terrible contradictions implicit in the story of Good Friday, the Spirit affirms both the reality of Jesus' death (with all its implications for the life of the first two persons) and the inability of death to conquer the love that unites and constitutes God as Father and Son. Though the Spirit is neither the Father nor the

Son, the fact that the Spirit does nothing other than confess the mutual love of the Father and the Son means that the Spirit does not stand over the first two persons of the Trinity as a higher God. Instead, the Spirit's office suggests (in line with John 4:24) that the Spirit is the mode in which the Father and the Son are God (in line with the traditional confessional formula that Jesus is the Son who reigns with the Father in the power of the Holy Spirit).

Crucially, however, this mode by which Jesus' relation to God is confirmed is not an end in itself, as though God's identity as the one who lives from the margins were exhausted in the relationship between the first two persons. Because the witness of the Spirit is realized concretely in the confession of human beings, it follows that the divine life itself is perfected only as it opens itself in the Spirit to the participation of that which is not divine. In other words, the God who commits the divine life to the marginalized in the person of Jesus Christ is finally vindicated as divine from the margins, as the Spirit bears witness to Jesus as the Son of the Father through the words and actions of those human creatures who live at the margins of God's own life. In this way (and for all its evident imperfections), the church's act of confession in the power of the Spirit is constitutive of God's own life and reign.

This is certainly not to equate the church with God in general or the Spirit in particular. But it does mean that the authority—and thus the identity—both of Christ and of the God he confesses is not something fixed above and beyond the vicissitudes of historical existence. It is rather a process of ongoing disclosure, the character and content of which continue to be functions of divine solidarity with the marginalized. This open-ended character of the divine identity does not mean that God is either more or other than the one Jesus called Father; on the contrary, it is a necessary implication of the claim that the one Jesus calls Father is God, since a defining feature of that identity as portrayed in the gospels is the refusal to hold that identity sacrosanct in the face of human suffering. Consequently, while Scripture leaves no doubt that a decisive test of the Holy Spirit's presence is its testimony to Jesus (1 Cor. 12:3; compare 1 John 4:2), it does not follow that such confession always requires the use of the terms "Father" and "Son."

Indeed, the claim that "Father" is the only acceptable designation for God disregards the fact that this same Father has declared otherwise by placing this identity in jeopardy in the ministry of the Son. By acting in this way, God has certainly not made the divine identity a plaything of human fancy. But God has made it clear that who God is cannot be stated independently of the perspective of the marginalized, since the identity God claims as the Father of the Son has as its essence the participation of the marginalized in God's own life. In other words, because the divine identity as Father and Son is confirmed only through a process whereby the persons named by these terms bind their lives (and thus their identities) to those who are farthest removed from them, the divine life itself belies any insistence upon these names as final or exclusive terms for naming God.[11]

Who then is God? For Christians, God is the one who was in Jesus Christ reconciling the world (2 Cor. 5:19). It follows that Christians cannot name God without telling the story of Jesus, and thereby describing relationships of sending (life), abandonment (death), and resurrection which that story entails.[12] But Christians cannot depend for the integrity of their telling of that story on the use of certain words, even words with the unimpeachable biblical pedigree of "Father," "Son," and "Spirit." For the identity of this God—precisely as that which has been revealed once and for all in Jesus Christ—is not something that can be accessed independently of those same poor with whom God has in Christ joined the divine destiny. *That* this God is named through Jesus is unavoidable so long as the church understands its mission as that of proclaiming the God of Jesus Christ. But *how* this God is named through Jesus will be determined only as the church struggles to tell Jesus' story as good news to the least, whom Jesus came to save and among whom he has pledged always to be found.

In light of this conclusion, there can be no objection in principle to ways of naming the triune God that do not involve the use of the terms "Father," "Son," and "Spirit." Whether any given alternative formulation is faithful to the story of Jesus Christ can only be decided on a case-by-case basis—but the same can and must also be said of the churches' traditional language for God.

Indeed, because God lives from the margins, the church arguably takes a greater risk when it adheres rigidly to established language for naming God than when it experiments with new ways of confessing God through the process of proclaiming Christ at its margins.[13] Because the church is the church of Jesus Christ, its practices are subject to constant testing in light of the community's encounter with the Spirit of Christ. And if, following Scripture, we identify that Spirit by its testimony to Christ come in the flesh (1 John 4:2), then we know that it is to be sought where the flesh of Jesus lived and died—on the margins.

To be sure, in the resurrection Jesus transcends the physical limitations of his former existence in space and time (see 2 Cor. 5:16). But the earthly path he traveled remains constitutive of his heavenly identity, such that those of us who remain on the hither side of death have no basis for supposing we can avoid this path and still reach the same goal—especially when Jesus himself expressly teaches otherwise (Matt. 10:38; 16:24 and pars.; compare 1 Cor. 1:23).[14] Jesus' own words of consolation and hope, as remembered by the apostles and recorded in the Scriptures, acquire their sense and power in the context of the fact that they were preached to the poor and despised of his day. We cannot pretend that our words retain the substance of his message—or even that they identify the same God he confessed—apart from commitment to the same social location. In the particular context of North America at the turn of the millennium, that commitment will require an openness to ways of naming God that emerge from the churches' encounters with the marginalized, especially those who suffer the multiple oppressions of gender, class, ethnicity, and sexual orientation.

CLAIMING AUTHORITY IN THE NAME OF GOD

The ability to name (and thus accurately identify) God is a necessary condition of the power to claim authority to speak in God's name. Recognition that the power of naming the God of Jesus Christ is bound up with commitment to the marginalized therefore demands a radical turn from the established modes by which authority traditionally has been exercised in the churches. This is not to suggest that the gospel is directed only to the marginalized or that God has nothing to do with those at the churches' center. Scripture is clear that God is no respecter of persons (Rom. 2:11; Eph. 6:9; Col. 3:25) and desires all to come to salvation (1 Tim. 2:4).

But the shape of our encounter with God cannot bypass the mode of God's encounter with us in Jesus of Nazareth. And (if the example of the scribes and priests of Jesus' day are any indication) Jesus' life and message probably will not seem like good news to those who shun the margins. Still worse, those who have difficulty hearing Jesus' message as good news may find it hard to resist the temptation to alter it so that it corresponds more nearly to their own criteria of goodness. In the process, the integrity of the gospel is destroyed not only for those at the church's center (who lull themselves into a false sense of security), but also for those at the margins (who quite understandably find themselves unable to see any good news in a message that simply reinforces the status quo).

Such attempts to reshape the gospel in order to buttress existing sociopolitical relations presupposes that theological authority can be claimed without reference to its origin in God's own way of being. They thereby run counter to the ways in which the divine life takes shape in and through the career of Jesus, culminating in the humanly mediated work of the Holy Spirit. From this perspective, it is clear that God's identity (and, therefore, God's authority) as Savior is not a datum that can be separated, even conceptually, from the concrete way in which God has determined to be Savior.

This being the case, the demand that the church exercise authority "from the outside in" should not be interpreted as just a specifically Christian way of responding to the widespread religious notion that God is essentially unknowable. The rationale for Christian focus on the marginalized is not human ignorance about God. In fact, just the opposite is the case: it is precisely because we have been given to know who God is in Jesus Christ that we are compelled to go to the margins in order to test our ways of speaking about God.[15] If Jesus, as the one to whom God has given "all authority on heaven and on earth" (Matt. 28:18), exercises authority from the margins of the covenant community, then Christians, too, must turn to the margins if they would claim this authority for their faith and practice.

In light of the way in which the life of the church, as lived from the outside in, serves as the medium through which the triune God constitutes the divine life, it should be clear that the church should not be regarded merely as an imperfect (if unavoidable) medium between ourselves and God. On the contrary, the church is the context in which the identity of the God who came among us in Jesus of Nazareth continues to be disclosed.

In the same way, divine freedom cannot be interpreted to mean that God lives independently of creation in general and humankind in particular. It must rather be interpreted in light of the concrete reality of God's refusal to be God apart from communion with humankind. It follows that questions like "Could God not have created?" and "Might God not have redeemed?" lose their object: if God's identity consists in having created and redeemed us, it is impossible to speak meaningfully of this God as though the work of creation and redemption had not taken place.[16] The fullness of the divine life is not merely revealed in the course of God's encounter with the world, but actually constituted in the course of that encounter, culminating in humanity's incorporation into the divine life through the sending of the Spirit.

This model of human participation in the divine life strikes against the idea that the perichoresis of the three divine persons serves as a model for human social relations. Human beings are not assigned the job of trying to imitate the divine life according to their own reduced capacity: to be burdened with the task of replicating the perfect mutuality of the Trinity would hardly qualify as gospel. The good news that Christians proclaim is just the opposite: that human beings have been freed from the impossible (and self-imposed) burden of trying to be "like God," because God has in Christ been revealed as one who is with and for us as we are, even to the extent of having bound the divine destiny to our own. The communion to which we are called is therefore not a pale reflection of the Trinity, but the life of the Trinity itself, which finds its own fullness as we come to share in it.[17]

In the same way that there are not two levels of being in communion, one human and the other divine, neither should the exercise of authority be conceived as a two-tiered system in which human activity is functionally distinct from a self-contained divine prototype. Just as God's own trinitarian life is fulfilled through the confessional activity of human beings in the power of the Spirit, so the participation of humankind is integral to God's way of exercising authority. God's authority as Sovereign is defined by the way in which God's own life takes shape through the mutual confession of the three divine persons.

Because this confession is fulfilled only as the Spirit inspires human beings to share in it, the authority Christians attribute to God cannot be divorced from the participation of human beings.[18] It follows that the relationship between divine and human authority should not be conceived in zero-sum terms. Since life in communion with that which is not God is both the mode and goal of God's exercise of authority, the endowing of human beings with authority implies the fulfillment rather than a diminution of divine authority.[19]

Consequently, for human beings to invoke this authority as a justification for lording it over others is not so much a misappropriation of God's authority as a failure to appropriate it at all. For the authority which is disclosed in the life, death, and resurrection of Jesus Christ is one that sides with the oppressed and, in doing so, exposes itself to the full power of sin and death. By overcoming this assault, God proves the divine self worthy of the trust of those who are similarly afflicted. Moreover, because God in victory has taken into the divine self the fullness of worldly defeat, the triumph of Easter does not leave the defeated behind but confirms their empowerment as the vanguard of God's own advent and reign.

It follows that all subsequent claims to divine authority must be measured by their ability to be heard as good news by those to whom the world has nothing good to say. For if the content of Jesus' message is inseparable from the response it elicited among the marginalized of his day, the fidelity of the churches' preaching depends on their ability to form themselves into communities capable of eliciting the same response by following a path of solidarity with the outcast.[20]

This does not mean that the church—let alone the God whose rule it proclaims—simply divests itself of authority. On the contrary, when Christians proclaim Jesus' resurrection in the power of the Spirit, they declare that the authority that seemed to go down to defeat on the cross is both real and ultimate. But precisely because this vindication comes through and beyond death (and, therefore, beyond the realm of human history), Jesus' claim to authority is defined by the fact that it does not ignore the suffering and pain or the sin and guilt which characterize historical existence. If in the resurrection—and thus from beyond history—Jesus claims authority in power, within history Jesus' authority is both claimed and constituted in weakness, from the place of the victim. It is real and ultimate authority because it surpasses and vanquishes death, but it is nonauthoritarian because it does so through death and thus in solidarity with even those aspects of human existence that are farthest removed from a position of power and security.

This authority demands the concrete obedience of disciples willing to take up their own crosses and follow where Jesus leads; but if we submit to this authority in the belief that it has been vindicated on the far side of death, we must also recognize that on the hither side it is an authority claimed from a position of powerlessness, by one who is himself subject to death. The same Jesus claims the same authority on both sides of the resurrection, but the side on which this Jesus stands makes a world of difference for the way in which this claim is made. In the earthly sphere, Jesus' (and, therefore, God's) authority is not manifested as power over history that is exercised in disregard of its vicissitudes, but as responsibility in history that is lived out through suffering and death. Indeed, because on the cross ultimate authority is severed from power within the sphere of history, the cross exposes all authority invoked in combination with power—whether that of the state, of science, or of religion—as bankrupt.

The implications of such a gospel are no less shocking today than they were in the first century. For they result in the seeming paradox that even Jesus (let alone the language Jesus uses) cannot be allowed to stand in the way of the hope that Jesus proclaims—and this precisely on the basis of Jesus' own refusal to count his divinity as more valuable than his mission of service to the realm of God (see Phil. 2:6–8). In other words, the identity of Jesus (and of the God whose reign he proclaims) is not a datum that can be viewed and assessed independently of the sum total of his encounters with particular people in particular situations.

It is not just that (as a matter of historical fact) Jesus is not known independently of the church, but that he cannot be: for Jesus' uniqueness and integrity, according to his divine no less than his human nature, lie in his work of proclaiming (and thereby inaugurating) God's realm at the margins of the covenant community. And to the extent that he is confessed as living still, his identity continues to be a function of his encounters with the marginalized as the church tells his story in the power of his Spirit.

To make this point is not to assert the priority of the church, the marginalized, or any other group as such over the reality of Jesus, but only to remind the church that Jesus has bound his reality to the fate of the oppressed.[21] The fundamental question for Christian theology is therefore not *who* has authority (as though authority were a quantity that could be possessed in the abstract) but *how* they have it. The mission of Jesus describes a model according to which authority is constituted only in its exercise "from the outside in." In this context, the charge of blasphemy falls rightly not on those who affirm the constitutive role of the oppressed in Christian theology, but on those whose attempts to separate Christ from the life of the marginalized amounts to a denial of the incarnation of the Word of God.

Different communities of Christians may be expected to appropriate the power of Jesus' ministry according to their own situation in the church and in society at large. But because the Risen One whose presence is the only compelling basis for any theological claim is also the crucified Jesus whose authority was exercised in responsibility to the least of those of his time and place, Christians of every situation find themselves pressed to acknowledge that the authority whereby they call others to responsibility has as its necessary condition that they themselves be responsible to their interlocutors.

The demand that Christians move to the margins of the church therefore does not mean that they should minimize their authority, in the sense that they should understand the faith they proclaim as only one of any number of equally viable options. On the contrary, Jesus asks Christians to take their authority with utmost seriousness as one which entails bearing news that is genuinely good to all people. But in order to do so they must recognize that this authority, far from releasing its claimants of responsibility to others, is defined by such responsibility. For if it is true that though heaven and earth should pass away, Jesus' words shall not, Jesus' own example shows that the meaning—and therefore the truth—of his words is not self-contained. Both alike are established only by way of his encounter with the least of his contemporaries, in whose presence the power and beauty of God's rule are realized. We who would be disciples and claim that authority are called to follow the same path. Only so can we, too, teach with authority and not as the scribes.

NOTES

INTRODUCTION

1. In this respect, I conceive my work as an example of the "ad hoc apologetics" described by George Lindbeck in *The Nature of Doctrine: Religion and Theology in a Postliberal Age* (Philadelphia: Westminster, 1984), 131.

1. THE PROBLEM OF AUTHORITY

1. This and subsequent translations of the New Testament are my own, except where otherwise indicated.

2. See the debate over the power by which Jesus casts out demons in Matt. 12:22–30 and pars., as well as the controversy surrounding the healing of the man born blind in John 9:13–16, 24–29.

3. Note that while Jesus does not offer such an account in Matt. 21, he does not call into question the right of his critics to raise the question; he merely demands that they be equally forthright. And the Gospel of John depicts Jesus going to some lengths to articulate the nature of his authority and its derivation from the one he calls Father (esp. John 5:31–40; 8:12–20).

4. See Matt. 26:53 and John 18:36 for biblical testimony to the effect that Jesus' willingness to be held accountable in this way is integral to the specific character of his authority.

5. To be sure, the church has been confronted by competing claims to authority from its inception, but it is only since the Enlightenment that the proliferation of competing claims in cultural settings where the authority of the church had been more or less taken for granted has caused the question of pluralism to emerge as a dominant motif in Western theology.

6. Thus, William Placher has recently attempted to bridge the gap between David Tracy's revisionist theology and George Lindbeck's postliberal approach in light of their common concern with issues raised by a pluralistic context (see William C. Placher, *Unapologetic Theology: A Christian Voice in a Pluralistic Conversation* (Louisville, Ky.: Westminster/John Knox Press, 1989), 20, 154–55.

7. Gustavo Gutiérrez, *A Theology of Liberation: History, Politics, and Salvation* (Maryknoll, N.Y.: Orbis, 1988), 11, 29–33. Compare the discussions of the rela-

tion between language and oppression in James Cone, *God of the Oppressed* (San Francisco: Harper & Row, 1974), 45–61; Leonardo Boff, *Liberating Grace* (Maryknoll, N.Y.: Orbis, 1979), 18–31; and Elisabeth Schüssler Fiorenza, *In Memory of Her: A Feminist Theological Reconstruction of Christian Origins* (New York: Crossroad, 1983), 3–6, 26–36.

8. See especially Wolfhart Pannenberg, *Systematic Theology* (Grand Rapids, Mich.: Eerdmans, 1991), vol. 1, sec. 4, where Pannenberg shows how, in the wake of the Reformation, Protestant orthodox attempts to justify faith claims by reference to a doctrine of the verbal inspiration of Scripture gave way to more-explicitly apologetic approaches to theological prolegomena in the later seventeenth and eighteenth centuries.

9. "Since the preliminary process of defining a science cannot belong to the science itself, it follows that none of the propositions which will appear in this [introduction] can themselves have a dogmatic character" (Friedrich Schleiermacher, *The Christian Faith*, ed. H. R. Mackintosh and J. S. Stewart [Edinburgh: T & T Clark, 1989], 2). Compare Schleiermacher's explanation: "Thus, the first part of our Introduction has only to collate and apply borrowed propositions, i.e. propositions which belong to other scientific studies, in this case to Ethics [Schleiermacher's term for what we might call social science], Philosophy of Religion, and Apologetics. Of course, the results of an investigation which is put together out of such component parts cannot lay claim to any general recognition, except when that form of Ethics and of the Philosophy of Religion which underlies the investigation is likewise recognized" (*The Christian Faith*, 5).

10. "The prefix pro in prolegomena is to be understood loosely to signify the first part of dogmatics rather than that which is prior to it" (Karl Barth, *Church Dogmatics* [hereafter *CD*], I.1, §2 [Edinburgh: T & T Clark, 1978], 42).

11. Ibid., I.1, §2, 43.

12. Ibid., I.1, §2, 331. Compare Jürgen Moltmann, *The Trinity and the Kingdom: The Doctrine of God*, trans. Margaret Kohl (San Francisco: Harper & Row, 1981), 140–41, who contrasts the Christological ground Barth attempts to give to his discussion of the Trinity in *CD* with the even more nakedly philosophical approach to the doctrine found in his *Christlicher Dogmatik im Entwurf* (1927).

13. In what may be regarded as the classic formulation of this argument, F. Gerald Downing has argued that, given the enormous diversity within Christianity with respect to both the formal question of how one determines what counts as revealed knowledge and the material question of what is in fact known, the meaning of the term "revelation" (which, in normal parlance, suggests a disclosure of information that is self-evident with respect to both its transmission and its content) needs to be so heavily qualified in theological contexts as to render its continuing use highly problematic (F. Gerald Downing, *Has Christianity a Revelation?* [London: SCM Press, 1964]). For a more specifically exegetical attack on the concept of revelation, see James Barr, *The Bible and the Modern World* (New York: Harper & Row, 1973), 120–32.

14. Ronald F. Thiemann, *Revelation and Theology: The Gospel as Narrated Promise* (Notre Dame, Ind.: University of Notre Dame Press, 1985), 2–7.

15. Ibid., 45–46.

16. "The problem is how to preserve authentic human agency while granting priority to God's action in the moment of revelation" (Thiemann, *Revelation and Theology*, 48).

17. Ibid., 71. Thiemann singles out the work of David Kelsey and Charles Wood

in particular on the ground that their purely functional view of scriptural authority undermines the idea of divine prevenience (*Revelation and Theology,* 67–69).

18. "Whatever their manifest flaws, modern doctrines of revelation have attempted to restate that central Christian conviction [that] . . . faith 'is not a human work but utterly a divine gift'" (Thiemann, *Revelation and Theology,* 3).

19. For example, the idea that two pieces cannot occupy the same square at the same time would be a "background belief" in chess. As Thiemann puts it, such beliefs "are basic because the coherence of many other beliefs depends on the acceptance of these beliefs as true, and they are background because their axiomatic status makes explicit justification of them unnecessary" (Thiemann, *Revelation and Theology,* 11).

20. Ibid., 14.

21. "When the assertion of God's prevenience [is allowed to] function as a background belief, a doctrine of revelation simply explicates the content of that knowledge given by God's grace" (Thiemann, *Revelation and Theology,* 11).

22. "Descriptive theology seeks to display the relation between belief in God's prevenience and the supporting and supported beliefs within the Christian faith, or failing in that task, it shows that such a belief cannot be sustained by the logic of Christian belief. The terms of the discussion of revelation within descriptive theology are thus substantially different from the epistemological and causal categories of foundational theology, but the problem of revelation, nonetheless, remains strikingly familiar" (Thiemann, *Revelation and Theology,* 78).

23. In an argument that parallels Thiemann's in many respects, Gustaf Wingren has criticized Barth for focusing on ignorance rather than sin as the problem that the gospel addresses. Wingren maintains that Barth's focus on the epistemological dynamics of revelation (noted above) leads him to interpret the gospel in terms of the communication of knowledge of God's (gracious) relationship to us rather than the act by which God effectively alters that relationship by forgiving the human violation of it. See Gustaf Wingren, *Theology in Conflict: Nygren–Barth–Bultmann,* trans. Eric H. Wahlstrom (Philadelphia: Muhlenberg Press, 1958), 110.

24. Thiemann, *Revelation and Theology,* 109.

25. Ibid., 110.

26. Ibid., 99–101.

27. As Thiemann notes, it is no more remarkable than the claim that "Little Red Riding Hood" functions to warn as well as to tell a story (*Revelation and Theology,* 103).

28. Thiemann, *Revelation and Theology,* 77.

29. This state of affairs appears all the more ironic when it is noted that Thiemann criticizes the functional conception of scriptural authority promoted by David Kelsey on the grounds that "while a functional conception of authority is surely compatible with belief in God's prevenience, it provides no positive support for that belief beyond the decisions of the theologians who hold it to be true" (Thiemann, *Revelation and Theology,* 64). As argued in the ensuing paragraphs, it is not easy to see why the decisions of the community as a whole (on which Thiemann bases his own argument) should be regarded as any less theologically problematic than that of individual theologians.

30. Thiemann, *Revelation and Theology,* 77–78.

31. Ibid., 76.

32. Ibid., 147.

2. THE CHURCH'S AUTHORITY AND CHRIST'S AUTHORITY

1. In this context, Augustine argued that the sacraments performed by the Donatist were valid but inefficacious. See "On Baptism," in *An Augustine Reader,* ed. John J. O'Meara (Garden City, N.Y.: Image Books, 1973), 207–9.

2. Interestingly, Augustine cites 1 Cor. 13:2 to argue that the latter sin is more serious than the former (see Augustine, "On Baptism," 217; cf. ibid., 219).

3. Augustine himself formulated the distinction between heresy and schism in the context of his controversy with the Donatists, whom he made a point of identifying as schismatics rather than heretics on the ground that they had broken with the catholic party over ethics rather than doctrine. (The Donatist churches refused to accept the validity of an ordination in which a bishop who had allegedly apostatized had participated.) As Augustine himself recognized, however, what began as an ethical question regarding the discipline of lapsed clergy in fact implied a whole theology in which the efficacy of sacramental acts was dependent on the personal merit of the officiant (*ex opere operantis*). Augustine repudiated this position as inconsistent with what was for him the fundamental truth that the efficacy of the sacraments was a matter of grace (specifically, the trustworthiness of Christ's promises to the community as a whole), and thus depended only on whether or not the sacramental act was performed in accordance with canonical requirements (*ex opere operato*).

4. This is, of course, not meant to deny the reality of schism as a distinct feature of church history but only to note that where schism has proved deep and lasting (e.g., between the Western and Eastern churches), it has generally been framed by both sides in explicitly dogmatic terms (e.g., in the question of the *filioque*).

5. Martin Luther, "Lectures on the Psalms," in *WA* 4.365; cited in John R. Loeschen, *The Divine Community: Trinity, Church, and Ethics in Reformation Theologies* (Kirksville, Mo.: Sixteenth Century Journal, 1981), 19.

6. "We confess that, although our Church is orthodox as far as her doctrine of grace is concerned, we are no longer sure we are members of the church which follows its Lord" (Dietrich Bonhoeffer, *The Cost of Discipleship* [New York: Macmillan, 1959], 60).

7. Ibid., 54–55.

8. Ibid., 50; cf. 69. One might also refer to Calvin's famous dictum that "not only faith, perfect and in every way complete, but all right knowledge of God is born of obedience" (John Calvin, *Institutes of the Christian Religion,* ed. John T. McNeil [Philadelphia: Westminster, 1960], I.vi.2, 72). While the obedience Calvin has in mind is quite specifically focused on subordination of the reason to Scripture, the point remains fundamentally the same as for Bonhoeffer: there is no possibility of evaluating the meaning of Christian teachings apart from active Christian discipleship.

9. Bonhoeffer, *Cost of Discipleship,* 81.

10. Thus, what the rich young man "expects from the good master [Jesus] is a weighty pronouncement, but certainly not a direction from God which would make an absolute claim on his obedience" (Bonhoeffer, *Cost of Discipleship,* 78).

11. Cone, *God of the Oppressed,* 113.

12. Compare Jon Sobrino's insistence both on the theological significance of the church's Christological dogmas and the need to interpret these dogmas in the context of the "living faith" of actual communities: "Although liberation christology knows and admits from the outset the truth of the dogmatic formulations, it insists on re-creating the process that led to them, *beginning with Jesus of Nazareth,*

and, further, holds that the re-creation of this process is the best way to come to an understanding of these formulas" (Jon Sobrino, *Jesus in Latin America* [Maryknoll, N.Y.: Orbis, 1987], 19, emphasis added).

13. The two poles of this debate are given classic form in E. Franklin Frazier, *The Negro Church in America* (New York: Schocken, 1964), and Melville Herskovits, *The Myth of the Negro Past* (Boston: Beacon, 1958). Frazier denies any significant survival of Africanisms among black Americans; Herskovits identifies a wide number of them. For an assessment of their respective views, see Albert J. Raboteau, *Slave Religion: The "Invisible Institution" in the Antebellum South* (New York: Oxford, 1978), 45–92, esp. 48–55.

14. Raboteau cites one such oath administered by Francis Le Jau, a missionary to slaves in South Carolina (*Slave Religion,* 123).

15. Raboteau observes: "Catechesis moved in two directions. The slaves were taught the prayers, doctrines, and rites of Christianity, but as the missionaries realized, the slaves had to somehow understand the meaning of Christian belief and ritual if instruction was to become more than mere parroting. And here the whites had only limited control. For the slaves brought their cultural past to the task of translating and interpreting the doctrinal words and ritual gestures of Christianity. Therefore the meaning which the missionary wished the slaves to receive and the meaning which the slaves actually found (or, better, made) were not the same" (*Slave Religion,* 126).

16. "Steal Away to Jesus" seems to have been used frequently to this end, while other spirituals (e.g., "Swing Low, Sweet Chariot") signaled that the Underground Railroad would be making a stop nearby (see Raboteau, *Slave Religion,* xx). It is also important to note that there is no need to invoke a hidden layer of meaning to appreciate the protest against the slave system found in spirituals like "Go Down, Moses" and "Oh Freedom!" For what remains the classic theological analysis of the spirituals as instruments of adaptation and protest, see James H. Cone, *The Spirituals and the Blues: An Interpretation* (San Francisco: Harper & Row, 1972).

17. This having been said, it must be added that public resistance to slavery was probably not as infrequent as has sometimes been suggested. Herbert Aptheker counts over 250 "reported Negro conspiracies and revolts" in the antebellum period (*Essays in the History of the American Negro* [New York: International, 1945], 11).

18. Erskine Clarke, *Wrestlin' Jacob: A Portrait of Religion in the Old South* (Atlanta: John Knox Press, 1984), 40; quoted from Emilie M. Townes, *In a Blaze of Glory: Womanist Spirituality as Social Witness* (Nashville, Tenn.: Abingdon, 1995), 27.

19. Compare, for example, the story of Uncle Silas, a venerable slave who reportedly challenged a white preacher's pie-in-the-sky talk of salvation with the repeated challenge, "[God] gonna give us freedom 'long wid salvation?" (Charles L. Perdue et al., eds., *Weevils in the Wheat: Interviews with Virginia Ex-slaves* [Bloomington: University of Indiana Press, 1980], 184; cited in Dwight N. Hopkins, *Shoes That Fit Our Feet: Sources for a Constructive Black Theology* [Maryknoll, N.Y.: Orbis, 1993], 27).

20. Although Jones was a racist and steadfastly defended slavery as an institution, he was also devoted to the cause of spreading Christianity among the slaves (which was regarded with extreme suspicion by and met with a corresponding lack of cooperation on the part of many slaveholders). If his goal had simply been to please masters, he could have accomplished his end much more easily by ignoring the slave altogether. See Charles Joyner, "'Believer I Know': The Emergence of

African-American Christianity," in *African-American Christianity: Essays in History,* ed. Paul E. Johnson [Berkeley: University of California Press, 1994], 22–25).

21. See, for example, the way in which Jesus forces the disciples to reevaluate the meaning of such terms in Matt. 16:21–23 and pars.; 18:1–5 and pars.; 19:30–20:16; 20:25–28 and pars.; 21:31b–32 and pars.

22. See Cone, *God of the Oppressed,* 123.

23. Gayraud Wilmore, "Black Theology: Review and Assessment," *Voices from the Third World* 5, no. 2 (1982): 14; compare Wilmore's discussion of the sources of black theology in *Black Religion and Black Radicalism* (Garden City, N.Y.: Doubleday, 1972), 298–300.

24. Cone, *God of the Oppressed,* 34; compare the following: "Because Black Theology has as its starting point the Black condition, this does not mean that it denies the absolute revelation of God in Christ. Rather, it means that Black theology firmly believes that God's revelation in Christ can be made supreme only by affirming Christ as he is alive in black people today" (James H. Cone, *Black Theology and Black Power* [New York: Seabury, 1968], 118).

25. Cone, *God of the Oppressed,* 35.

26. "Th[e] vertical sense of personal relationship with the God of Jesus is logically prior to the other components of human liberation. For without the knowledge of God that comes through divine fellowship, the oppressed would not know that what the world says about them is a lie" (Cone, *God of the Oppressed,* 143).

27. James H. Cone, *A Black Theology of Liberation: Twentieth Anniversary Edition* (Maryknoll, N.Y.: Orbis, 1990), 12.

28. "Though my perspective begins with humanity, it is not humanity in general . . . [but] oppressed humanity. In America that means black humanity. This is the point of departure for black theology, because it believes that oppressed humanity is the point of departure for Christ himself" (Cone, *Black Theology of Liberation,* 19).

29. Cone writes: "The history of white American theology illustrates the concept of the social a priori asserted by Werner Stark and the other sociologists of knowledge. . . . The[ir] social environment functions as a 'mental grid,' deciding what will be considered as relevant data in any given inquiry. . . . Because white theologians were not enslaved and lynched and are not ghettoized because of color, they do not think that color is an important point of departure for theological discourse. Color is not *universal,* they say, moving on to what they regard as the more important problems of theological scholarship. [But] universalism is a social product and it remains such even (especially!) when it is legitimized in pious or scholarly language" (Cone, *God of the Oppressed,* 52–53).

30. Ibid., 58; compare the following: "The dissimilarity between Black theology and white theology lies at the point of each having different mental grids which account for their different approaches to the gospel" (Cone, *God of the Oppressed,* 45).

31. Cone, *Black Theology of Liberation,* 61.

32. Cone states: "What whites fail to recognize is the fact that all decisions made with regard to what is important or worthwhile are made in the context of participation in a community. . . . [Thus] if whites expect to be able to say anything relevant to the self-determination of the black community, it will be necessary for them to destroy their whiteness [i.e., their privilege as the bearers of established authority] by becoming members of the oppressed community" (*Black Theology of Liberation,* 97).

33. Cone, *God of the Oppressed,* 147.

34. Cone, *Black Theology of Liberation,* 19.

35. See ibid., xv–xvi.

36. To be sure, Cone rejects white theologians' claims to sit in judgment on the black church, but even this stance is a theological decision that is defended through extended analysis of the history and practice of the white churches. Furthermore, the space that Cone devotes to responding to the concerns of his white critics suggests that he gives the claims of traditional theology somewhat more weight in practice than he appears to concede in theory.

3. THE CHURCH'S AUTHORITY AND THE PRIORITY OF SCRIPTURE

1. For example, some Christians view the office of bishop as part of Christ's constitution of the church; others view it as the church's own creation and thus subject to assessment in light of the community's needs and circumstances.

2. Luther wrote to Erasmus: "It is on this account that I have hitherto attacked the pope, in whose kingdom nothing is more commonly stated or more generally accepted, than the idea that the Scriptures are obscure or ambiguous, so that the spirit to interpret them must be sought from the Apostolic See of Rome. Nothing more pernicious could be said than this, for it has led ungodly men to set themselves above the Scriptures and to fabricate whatever they pleased, until the Scriptures have been completely trampled down" (Martin Luther, "On the Bondage of the Will," in *Luther and Erasmus: Free Will and Salvation* [Philadelphia: Westminster, 1969], 158–59).

3. Formula of Concord (Epitome, "Rule and Norm," 1) in *The Book of Concord: The Confessions of the Evangelical Lutheran Church* (Philadelphia: Muhlenberg, 1959), 464–65.

4. This position was explicitly formulated at the Council of Trent: "To restrain irresponsible minds, [the Council] decrees that no one, relying on his own prudence, twist Holy Scripture in matters of faith and morals that pertain to the edifice of Christian doctrine, according to his own mind, contrary to the meaning that holy mother the Church has held and holds—since it belongs to her to judge the true meaning and interpretation of Holy Scripture" (*DS* 1507). This last point is clarified by the Second Vatican Council: "Sacred Scripture must be read and interpreted in the same spirit in which it was written. In order therefore to discover the correct meaning of the sacred texts, no less serious attention must be paid to the content and the unity of the whole of Scripture in the light of the living Tradition of the whole Church and of the analogy of faith" (*Dei Verbum,* III.12). Citations are taken from J. Neuner and J. Dupuis, eds., *The Christian Faith in the Doctrinal Documents of the Catholic Church* (New York: Alba House, 1982), 75, 90.

5. Luther, of course, also held that illumination by the Holy Spirit was "necessary for every individual Christian" as that means by which one "is enlightened concerning himself and his own salvation." But he sharply distinguished this "internal" clarity of Scripture from what he took to be the fundamental principle that the Word of God, as publicly proclaimed, is accessible to all, regardless of whether they come to believe in it or not. See Luther, "On the Bondage of the Will," 159.

6. Luther, for example, argued that the church "condemns a heretic, not according to its own discretion, but . . . according to Holy Scripture, which they confess to be the law of the holy church." Consequently, "we must have something else and something more for our faith than the councils [and, by implica-

tion, any source of church tradition]. That 'something else' and 'something more' is Holy Scripture" (Martin Luther, "On the Councils and the Church," in *Church and Ministry, III,* vol. 41 of *Luther's Works* [Philadelphia: Fortress, 1966], 133, 120). Similarly, Calvin observed that "a most pernicious error widely prevails that Scripture has only so much weight as is conceded to it by the consent of the church. As if the eternal and inviolable truth of God depended upon the decision of men! . . . Yet, if this is so, what will happen to miserable consciences seeking firm assurance of eternal life if all promises of it consist in and depend solely upon the judgment of men? Will they cease to vacillate and tremble when they receive such an answer?" (*Institutes,* I.vii.1, 75).

7. "For it ought to be settled and established among Christians that the Holy Scriptures are a spiritual light far brighter than the sun itself, especially in things that are necessary to salvation" (Luther, "On the Bondage of the Will," 159).

8. Ibid., 162.

9. Indeed, because he understands the gospel as properly oral in character, Luther views the Bible's existence as text as lamentable, if unavoidable: "It is not the New Testament way, to write books about Christian doctrine, but there should be everywhere, without books, good, learned, spiritual, zealous preachers, who should draw out the living word from the ancient [Old Testament] Scriptures, and unceasingly exhort preachers as the Apostles did. For before they wrote they had first preached to the people with actual words and converted them, and this was their real Apostolic and New Testament work. . . . But that it should be necessary to write books was a great loss and failure of the Spirit; it was the result of compulsion, and not the matter of the New Testament" (cited in Gerhard Ebeling, "'Sola Scriptura' and Tradition," in *The Word of God and Tradition: Historical Studies Interpreting the Divisions of Christianity* [Philadelphia: Fortress, 1968], 112).

10. Luther "On the Bondage of the Will," 159.

11. On the contrary, Luther explicitly notes that "this inability of [Christ's] adversaries to withstand [the witness of Scripture] does not mean that they are compelled to abandon their own position, or are persuaded either to confess or to keep silence." The point is that this failure to recognize the truth is grounded in the obstinacy of the human heart, not in any obscurity of the biblical witness (Luther, "On the Bondage of the Will," 163; see also ibid., 167).

12. Käsemann states: "The New Testament canon does not, as such, constitute the foundation of the unity of the Church. On the contrary, as such (that is, in its accessibility to the historian) it provides the basis for the multiplicity of the confessions. The variability of the kerygma in the New Testament is an expression of the fact that in primitive Christianity a wealth of different confessions were already in existence, constantly replacing each other. . . . It is thus quite comprehensible that the confessions which exist today all appeal to the New Testament canon. Fundamentally, the exegete cannot dispute their methodological or their material right to do so" (Ernst Käsemann, "The Canon of the New Testament and the Unity of the Church," in *Essays on New Testament Themes,* vol. 41 of *Studies in Biblical Theology* [London: SCM, 1964], 103–4).

13. Ernst Käsemann, "Thoughts on the Present Controversy about Scriptural Interpretation," in *New Testament Questions of Today* (Philadelphia: Fortress, 1969), 262.

14. "The following formulation of the position is extremely dangerous, but we need this kind of exaggeration today: it is the Spirit alone who makes possible a critical and proper hearing of Scripture. . . . Nothing is 'Spirit' which does not set us

within the righteousness of faith, i.e., the justification of the ungodly" (Käsemann, "Thoughts," 271).

15. Ebeling, *"Sola Scriptura,"* 143–44.

16. Ebeling states: "The Roman Catholic interpretation of the canon, which in the last analysis anchors the authority of the canon to an ecclesiastical decree, can therefore only admit the canonicity of Scripture as subject to a tradition of interpretation. The Reformers' interpretation of the canon, on the other hand, which allows its authority to depend on the collection of writings accepted as canonical, can only accept the ecclesiastical decree as canonical in the sense that, as interpretation, it is tested by Scripture itself, and thus bound to the Word in its judgment about the canonicity of Scripture" (*"Sola Scriptura,"* 121).

17. Ebeling continues: "The fact that they are the sole source of revelation is only fully grasped when it is understood that they are the sole source of their interpretation, and that as such they do not need another source for it" (*"Sola Scriptura,"* 127).

18. Ebeling observes: *"Sola scriptura* only fulfills its essential function in the following ways: it preserves intact the proper distinction between text and interpretation; while the Catholic conception is in danger of ascribing to an interpretation the value of an authoritative text. Next, *sola scriptura* maintains that the Word of God has absolute priority over the Church as brought into existence by the Word of God, and therefore that the Church itself is not the authoritative source of the Word of God" (*"Sola Scriptura,"* 136).

19. Ebeling argues: "When we consider Scripture from the point of view of historical criticism, it seems to add to our difficulties that the one *traditum tradendum* [Christ] should have reached us only in the form of various oral and doctrinal traditions . . . but it is this that points to the decisive fact that the content of the *traditum tradendum* is not a doctrinal statement, nor a law, nor a book of Revelation, but the very Person of Jesus . . . as the incarnate Word of God" (*"Sola Scriptura,"* 146).

20. See, for example, Karl Rahner, *Foundations of Christian Faith: An Introduction to the Idea of Christianity,* trans. William V. Dych (New York: Crossroad, 1978), 360–65.

21. For example, Cone argues: "This is an important matter, and perhaps the place to begin for clarification is to state emphatically that, like Scripture, the black experience is a source of the Truth but not the Truth itself. Jesus Christ is the Truth and thus stands in judgment over all statements about the truth. But having said that, we must immediately balance it with another statement, without which the first statement falsifies what it intends to affirm. We must state the other side of the paradox emphatically: There is no truth in Jesus Christ independent of the oppressed of the land—their history and culture" (Cone, *God of the Oppressed,* 33).

22. Ibid., 113.

23. In this context, Cone maintains that "universalism is a social product and it remains such even (especially!) when it is legitimized in pious or scholarly language" (*God of the Oppressed,* 53).

24. "Because the sociopolitical framework of [white] consciousness has been shaped already by white sociopolitical interests, their exposition of the problem of faith in history is limited to defending the intellectual status of religious claims against erosion by historical criticism. . . . sharing the consciousness of the Enlightenment, [white theologians] failed to question the consequences of the so-called enlightened view as reflected in colonization and slavery" (Cone, *God of the Oppressed,* 45–46).

25. "Both [Luther and Calvin] would have agreed that if one has to choose between the subject matter and the words of a biblical text, one obviously opts for the former.... But for both the important fact was that the choice between subject matter and text was in effect secondary and a matter of edifying corrective rather than distinction in principle" (Hans W. Frei, *The Eclipse of Biblical Narrative: A Study in Eighteenth and Nineteenth Century Hermeneutics* [New Haven, Conn.: Yale University Press, 1974], 23).

26. Ibid., 280; compare the following: "Literal depiction constitutes and does not merely illustrate or point to the meaning of the narrative and theme it cumulatively renders; and simultaneously it depicts and renders the reality (if any) of what it talks about" (ibid., 27).

27. Frei, *Types of Christian Theology* (New Haven, Conn.: Yale University Press, 1992), 84.

28. Frei traces this development to the latter half of the eighteenth century: "The explicative meaning of the narrative texts came to be their ostensive or ideal reference. Their applicative meaning or religious meaningfulness was either a truth of revelation embodied in an indispensable historical event or a universal spiritual truth known independently of the texts but exemplified by them" (Frei, *Eclipse,* 124).

29. Ibid., 127.

30. Cone observes: "It is as if blacks have intuitively drawn the all-important distinction between infallibility and reliability. They have not contended for a full and explicit infallibility, feeling perhaps that there is mystery in the Book, as there is in Christ. What they have testified to is the Book's reliability: how it is the true and basic source for discovering the truth of Jesus Christ. For this reason there has been no crisis of scriptural authority in the black community. The Jesus of black experience is the Christ of Scripture, the One who was born in Bethlehem, grew up in Nazareth, taught in Galilee, and died and was resurrected in Jerusalem" (*God of the Oppressed,* 111–12). Compare the proposal for reading the Bible from a Hispanic perspective in Justo L. Gonzalez, *Mañana: Christian Theology from a Hispanic Perspective* (Nashville, Tenn.: Abingdon, 1990), 86–87.

31. Ebeling, *"Sola Scriptura,"* 144.

32. In this context Ebeling remarks: "If the inseparable connection between Scripture and Church, Scripture and Tradition is understood to mean that Scripture does not exist in isolation in the form of a book, but is transmitted in the activity of preaching, not in order that it may remain in written form as "Holy Scripture," but to serve as an aid to preaching, and to constitute its subject as the preacher's text, then there need be no dispute about sola scriptura" (*"Sola Scriptura,"* 116).

33. Richard B. Hays, *Echoes of Scripture in the Letters of Paul* (Philadelphia: Westminster, 1989), 102.

34. Frei explains: "With few exceptions, the theologians (and philosophers of religion who have wanted to make a case for Christianity) have been preoccupied ever since the beginning of the eighteenth century with showing the credibility or (in our day) the 'meaningfulness' of Christianity to their skeptical or confused contemporaries. Certain basic patterns appear repeatedly in this apologetic procedure.... Whatever my convictions about the uses of apologetics in Christian thought, the present essay ... affirms a sharp distinction between 'meaning' in dogmatic theology and such apologetic interpretations of the Christian faith. It is an inquiry into one sort of basis for dogmatic theology and as such

ignores apologetical issues" (Hans W. Frei, *The Identity of Jesus Christ: The Hermeneutical Bases of Dogmatic Theology* [Philadelphia: Fortress, 1975], xi–xii).

35. Frei explains: "It will be evident that this exercise of ordering and praise, involving neither new evidence for the truth of Christian faith nor the development of fresh claims based on prior statements, is in one perspective an empty exercise. That is to say, it is a purely formal and circular procedure, an exercise in clarification, adding no new information and providing no new conclusions. In other words, we talk about the relation to Christ as if it were already established and simply wanted a kind of descriptive expansion" (*Identity*, 5).

36. Ibid., 6.

37. "Even if our knowledge of a given person's identity does not depend on or require [that person's] specific and physical presence, every time we think of him there is a sense in which that person is 'present' . . . through the aid of memory and imagination." Even in this weak sense, however, "the imagination, or the person doing the imagining, is *not forced* into uniting the content of the imagination with the grasp of *actual* presence" (Frei, *Identity*, 15).

38. Ibid., 146.

39. Ibid.

40. This is not to deny that the results of historical-critical research (or, in another age, allegorical interpretation) might provide insight into the community's understanding of Scripture; it is only to point out that such data are not in themselves constitutive of Christian claims about Jesus.

41. "The realistic or history-like quality of the narrative, whether historical or not, prevents even the person who regards the account as implausible from regarding it as mere myth. Rather, it is to him a kind of hyperfiction claiming to be self-warranting fact" (Frei, *Identity*, 143).

42. Frei argues: "There may or may not be a class called 'realistic narrative,' but to take it as a general category of which the synoptic Gospel narratives . . . are a dependent instance is first to put the cart before the horse and then to cut the lines and claim the vehicle is self-propelled. The realistic novel . . . is, from the perspective of the rule of faith and its interpretive use in the Christian tradition, nothing more than an appropriate even if puzzling as well as incomplete analogy or 'type' of their 'antitype' . . . in the Gospel stories" (Hans W. Frei, "The 'Literal Reading' of the Biblical Narrative in the Christian Tradition: Does It Stretch or Will It Break?" in *Theology and Narrative: Selected Essays* [New York: Oxford, 1993], 142–43).

43. Thus, in a later essay, Frei notes that "there is no a priori reason why the 'plain' reading [in the Christian tradition] could not have been 'spiritual' in contrast to 'literal,' and certainly the temptation was strong. The identification of the plain with the literal sense was not a logically necessary development, but it did begin with the early Christian communities and was perhaps unique to Christianity" ("'Literal Reading,'" 122); compare the following: "the literal meaning of the text is precisely that meaning which finds the greatest degree of agreement in the use of the text in the religious community" (Frei, *Types*, 15).

44. Frei, *Identity*, 137.

45. Frei explains: "The relationship between the church and Jesus Christ is somewhat like that between Israel and Jesus. To describe the people of Israel is to narrate its history. And to identify that people . . . with the identity of Jesus Christ is to narrate the history of Jesus . . . in such a way that it is seen as the individual and climactic summing up, incorporation and identification of the whole people. . . . The

church likewise moves toward an as yet undisclosed historical summing up that must be narrated, though it cannot yet be because the story is unfinished" (*Identity,* 159).

Compare Barth's observation: "The reason why the establishment of the community by Jesus himself does not emerge as a definite and distinctive event in the Gospel tradition is that this is the theme of the whole Gospel narrative as an account of Jesus, the whole of the Gospel narrative as an account of Jesus necessarily being an account of the birth of the Christian community, of the development, corresponding to and consummating the unification of the twelve tribes of Israel in the exodus from Egypt, of the people of God of the last time which has been inaugurated with the coming of Jesus Christ" (*CD,* IV.3.ii, 683).

46. As Frei notes, this does not mean that Jesus is present only in the church, but it does mean that Jesus is only acknowledged as present there: "the church is simply the witness to the fact that it is Jesus Christ and none other who is the ultimate presence in and to the world" (Frei, *Identity,* 158–59).

47. Hays, *Echoes,* 168.

4. THE POLITICS OF THEOLOGY AND THE CHURCH'S IDENTITY

1. In this context, it is worth noting that those in authority do not stand for God, but for the community as the object of God's ongoing commitment and concern.

2. This point is made with particular force by Dietrich Bonhoeffer: "God's gracious will should be specially recognized in a national church [*Volkskirche*], in that as an organically developed historical power it possesses greater firmness and lasting power than a voluntary association: historically sterile periods can be withstood by the national church, whereas the gathered church [*Freiwilligkeitskirche*] is ruined by such a time. It is divine grace that we have a church which is deeply rooted in the history of the nation, which makes the divine will for us, given through the power of the church's historicity, relative[ly] independent of the momentary human situation" (Dietrich Bonhoeffer, *The Communion of Saints: A Dogmatic Inquiry into the Sociology of the Church* [New York: Harper & Row, 1963], 187–88).

3. Bonhoeffer states: "In view of all we have said, especially of the necessity of the national church from a dogmatic standpoint, we can now affirm . . . that a national church, which is not continually pressing forward to be a confessing church, is in the greatest inner peril. There is a moment when the church dare not continue to be a national church, and this moment has come when the national church can no longer see how it can win its way through to being a gathered church . . . but on the contrary is moving into complete emptiness and petrification" (*Communion of Saints,* 189–90).

4. Thus Augustine notes that "the church has often been only in one individual, or in one family" (*Enarrationes in Psalmos,* 128.2, cited in Bonhoeffer, *Communion of Saints,* 148).

5. The Great Schism had, of course, posed the question of the identity of the true church in the West, but the problem of multiple popes was not primarily one of multiple communions with distinct theologies and liturgies. In the same way, the conciliar movement of the fourteenth and fifteenth centuries focused primarily on the structure and organization of the one church, not with the practical question of evaluating the ecclesial status of two or more distinct ecclesiastical bodies. The questions raised by the Hussite movement are far closer to those of the Reformation (and the Huss was recognized by the Reformers as an important precursor to their own

struggles), but its immediate theological impact was limited by virtue of its location on the periphery of the church and its relative geographical isolation.

6. Luther explains that "the Children's Creed teaches us . . . that a Christian holy people is to be and to remain on earth until the end of the world. This is an article of faith that cannot be terminated until that which it believes comes. . . . But how will or how can a poor confused person tell where such a Christian holy people are to be found in this world?" ("On the Councils and the Church," in *Church and Ministry*, III, vol. 41 of *Luther's Works,* ed. Eric W. Gritsch [Philadelphia: Fortress Press, 1966], 148).

7. Calvin explains: "Holy Scripture speaks of the church in two ways. Sometimes by the term 'church' it means that which is actually in God's presence, into which no persons are received but those who are the children of God by grace of adoption and true members of the church by sanctification of the Holy Spirit. Then, indeed, the church includes not only the saints presently living, but all the elect from the beginning of the world. Often, however, the name 'church' designates the whole multitude of men spread over the earth who profess to worship one God and Christ. . . . In this church are mingled many hypocrites who have nothing of Christ but the name and outward appearance" (*Institutes,* IV.i.7, 1021).

8. Apology of the Augsburg Confession, Art. VII–VIII, in *BC,* 169; compare question 100 from the Geneva Catechism: "M. Can this [invisible] Church of God be known in any other way than by believing in her? C. There is indeed the visible Church of God, for the recognition of which [God] has certain signs, but here we speak properly of the fellowship of those whom He has elected to salvation which cannot be seen plainly by the eye" (*The Proposed Book of Confessions of the Presbyterian Church in the United States* [hereafter *BOC*] [(n.p.), 1976], 19).

9. See, for example, the Apology of the Augsburg Confession, Art. VII–VIII: "Christ has also warned us in his parables on the church that when we are offended by the personal conduct of priests or people, we should not incite schisms" (in *The Book of Concord: The Confessions of the Evangelical Lutheran Church,* trans. and ed. Theodore G. Tappert [Philadelphia: Muhlenberg Press, 1959], 178); and the Westminster Confession, XXVII.4–5: "The purest churches under heaven are subject both to mixture and error, and some have so degenerated as to become apparently no churches of Christ. Nevertheless, there shall be always a church on earth, to worship God according to his will" (*BOC,* 96). (Cf. Augsburg Confession, Art. VIII in *BC,* 33; the Formula of Concord [Epitome, Art. XII.7], in *BC,* 498; and Calvin, *Institutes,* IV.i.10, 1024–5.)

10. Thus, much to Melanchthon's frustration, the authors of the Roman Confutation suggested that the Augsburg Confession promoted a crypto-Donatism, arguing that the Lutheran claim "that the church is the assembly of saints cannot be admitted without prejudice to the faith if by this definition the wicked and sinners are separated from the church" (*BC,* 168, n. 1).

11. Nor was this simply a matter of trading accusations, for the Reformers contended that the combination of ecclesial triumphalism and theological indifference exhibited by the contemporary Roman hierarchy was proof of the urgency of their concern. Even the normally irenic Melanchthon could be quite biting on this issue: "Perhaps our opponents demand some such definition of the church as the following. It is the supreme outward monarchy of the whole world in which the Roman pontiff must have unlimited power beyond question or censure. . . . If we defined the church in that way, we would probably have fairer judges" (Apology, Art. VII–VIII, *BC,* 172–73).

12. Ibid., 171–72.

13. See above, 43–44.

14. Compare questions 305–6 from the Geneva Catechism: M. Do you mean that it is not enough for people to read [Scripture] privately at home, without altogether hearing its teaching in common? C. That is just what I mean . . . because Jesus Christ has established this order in His Church (Eph. 4:11), and He has declared this to be the only means of edifying and preserving it. Thus we must keep ourselves to it and not be wiser than our master" (*BOC,* 37).

15. "As we believe and confess the Scriptures of God sufficient to instruct and make perfect the man of God, so do we affirm and avow that their authority is from God, and . . . that they who say the Scriptures have no other authority save that which they have received from the Kirk are blasphemous against God and injurious to the true Kirk" (Scots Confession, Ch. XIX, *BOC,* 53).

16. Formula of Concord (Solid Declaration, "Rule and Norm"), in *BC,* 504.

17. Scots Confession, Ch. XX, in *BOC,* 54.

18. The authors of the Lutheran Formula of Concord stressed this point: "[Our] doctrine, drawn from and conformed to the Word of God, is summarized in the articles and chapters of the Augsburg Confession against the aberrations of the papacy and other sects. We therefore declare our adherence to the first, unaltered Augsburg Confession . . . as our symbol in this epoch, not because this confession was prepared by our theologians but because it is taken from the Word of God and solidly and well grounded therein. This symbol distinguishes our reformed churches from the papacy and from other condemned sects and heresies" (*BC,* 504).

19. Once again, the Formula of Concord bears testimony to this fact, being presented as a "Thorough, Pure, Correct, and Final Restatement and Explanation of a Number of Articles of the Augsburg Confession on Which for Some Time There Has Been Disagreement among Some Theologians Adhering to this Confession" (*BC,* 463).

20. See note 12 above, as well as the formulation in the Augsburg Confession, Art. VII (*BC,* 32), on which it is based.

21. "Wherever we see the Word of God purely preached, and the sacraments administered according to Christ's institution, there, it is not to be doubted, a church of God exists" (Calvin, *Institutes,* IV.i.9, 1023).

22. Scots Confession, Ch. XVIII, in *BOC,* 52.

23. Luther, "On the Councils," 148–65.

24. "The holy Christian people are externally recognized by the holy possession of the sacred cross [i.e., t]hey must endure every misfortune and persecution, all kinds of trial and evil from the devil, the world, and the flesh" (Luther, "On the Councils," 164).

25. "No intelligent person will quibble about the number of sacraments or the terminology, so long as those things are kept which have God's command and promises" (Apology of the Augsburg Confession, Art. XIII, in *BC,* 213).

26. See especially the Augsburg Confession, Art. VII, XIV–XV.

27. Here the Lutheran response to the Roman Catholic position on the sacramental character of ordination, which also reflects an insistence on a particular form of church order, applies equally to the Reformed camp: "If ordination is interpreted in relation to the ministry of the Word, we have no objection to calling ordination a sacrament. . . . The church has the command to appoint min-

isters; to this we must subscribe wholeheartedly, for we know that God approves this ministry and is present in it" (Apology, Art. XIII, in *BC,* 212).

28. "Two things are necessary for the right administration of the sacraments. The first is that they should be ministered by lawful ministers, and we declare that these are men appointed to preach the Word, unto whom God has given the power to preach the gospel, and who are lawfully called by some Kirk" (Scots Confession, Ch. XXII, in *BOC,* 55).

5. CHRISTIAN CONFESSION AND THE IDENTITY OF JESUS CHRIST

1. See also John 12:26: "If anyone would serve me, let him follow me, and where (*'opou*) I am, there (*ekei*) also will my servant be." Compare the following: "In the same way, moreover, many of the leaders also believed in [Jesus], but on account of the Pharisees they did not confess [*'omologoun*] him, lest they should be put out of the synagogue; for they loved human glory more than the glory of God" (John 12:42–43).

2. Thus, even the human rejection of Jesus presupposes a prior action on his part. The fact that such rejection remains a possibility for human beings is simply corollary to the fact that the relationship to which Jesus invites us is based in freedom, not necessity or compulsion.

3. The account in John is richer in detail but not much different with respect to overall impression: "Then Pilate went again into the garrison and called Jesus and said to him, 'Are you the king of the Jews?' Jesus answered, 'Do you say this on your own behalf, or have others spoken to you about me?' Pilate answered, 'Am I a Jew? Your own people and leaders have handed you over to me. What have you done?' Jesus answered, 'My realm is not from this world. If my realm were from this world, my servants would fight for me, so that I would not be handed over to the Jews. But my realm is not from here.' Then Pilate said to him, 'So you are a king?' Jesus answered, 'You say that I am a king. For this I was born and for this I came into the world, so that I might witness to the truth; everyone who belongs to the truth hears my voice.' Pilate said to him, 'What is truth?' " (John 18:33–38; cf. 19:9–11).

4. The fact that the presence of the God who Jesus proclaims is not bound up with the established authorities does not, of course, mean that God necessarily stands against them. While the author of Revelation does see the God of Jesus Christ implacably opposed to the worldly order established by the Antichrist, the balance of the New Testament makes it clear that this opposition cannot be regarded as the norm. Both Peter and Paul counsel deference to worldly authority (Rom. 13:1–7; 1 Pet. 2:13–17), and Luke in particular goes out of his way to argue that Christianity is no threat to Roman rule (not the least in his depiction of Pilate; see Luke 23:20–22; cf. Acts 23:29; 26:31). The fact remains, however, that the authorities' own conceptions of power make it difficult for them to view the realm Jesus proclaims as anything other than a threat.

5. Attempting to make sense of this fact in the context of the doctrine of the atonement, Gerhard Forde notes that according to Hebrews 13:10–12, Christ's work culminates not at the altar (the official center of the cult), but "outside the gate," where the refuse is burned ("The Work of Christ," in *Christian Dogmatics,* vol. 2, ed. Carl E. Braaten and Robert W. Jenson [Philadelphia: Fortress, 1984], 85–86).

6. Sobrino has made this point particularly well: "For Jesus becoming incarnate did not mean setting himself in the totality of history so as to correspond to the totality of God from there; it meant rather choosing that particular spot in

history that was capable of leading him to the totality of God. This spot is none other than that of the poor and oppressed" (*Jesus in Latin America,* 134).

7. I concur with Elisabeth Schüssler Fiorenza that the category of "the poor" is by itself too narrow to describe the inclusive character of Jesus' ministry. "Added to this category must be that of 'the marginal,' because the healing stories . . . indicate that Jesus and his movement were open to all, especially 'the outcast' of his society and religion. Although the majority of tax collectors, prostitutes, and sinners may have been poor, some of them probably were not" (Fiorenza, *In Memory of Her,* 141).

8. It is perhaps worth noting in this context that the Jesus of the Gospels is almost never identified with non-Jews, notwithstanding his occasional encounters with Samaritans and Gentiles (for a significant exception, see John 8:48). In this way, even his opponents recognize that his mission is directed to Israel—albeit to the "lost sheep" on its margins.

9. As James Cone puts it: "God's election of oppressed Israelites has unavoidable implications for the doing of theology. If God had chosen as his 'holy nation' the Egyptian slave masters instead of the Israelite slaves, then a completely different kind of God would have been revealed. Thus Israel's election cannot be separated from her servitude and liberation. . . . The doing of theology, therefore, on the basis of the revelation of Yahweh, must involve the politics which takes its stand with the poor and against the rich" (*God of the Oppressed,* 65).

10. Cone takes special note of this fact in *God of the Oppressed,* 68–70.

11. To be sure, when Saul is officially declared king, it is said that "when he took his stand among the people, he was head and shoulders taller than any of them" (1 Sam. 10:23); similarly, David "was ruddy, and had beautiful eyes, and was handsome" (1 Sam. 16:12). Yet neither was viewed as a likely candidate to start with: Saul had to be fetched from the baggage and David from the sheepfold (1 Sam. 10:21–22; 16:11).

12. In Matthew, for example (cf. the parallels in Mark and Luke), we have a leper (8:2), a centurion (8:10), the Gadarene demoniacs (8:29), a paralytic (9:2), the woman with the hemorrhage (9:22), two blind men (9:29), the Canaanite woman (15:28), the woman who anoints Jesus in the house of Simon (26:13), and the centurion at the cross (27:54). To this list (taken from Ronald Thiemann's essay "Radiance and Obscurity in Biblical Narratives," in *Constructing a Public Theology: The Church in a Pluralistic Culture* [Louisville, Ky.: Westminster/John Knox Press, 1991, 57]), we might add the Samaritan leper (Luke 17:16–19), Zacchaeus (Luke 19:8–9), the repentant thief (Luke 23:42), the Samaritan woman (John 4:39), the man born blind (John 9:38), and Martha of Bethany (John 11:27).

13. In line with this point, it is worth noting Jesus' inability/reluctance to perform miracles where he is not recognized in faith (Matt. 13:53–58 and pars.).

14. Indeed, in what Luke portrays as his first public sermon, Jesus makes a point of noting that God's salvific activity is not limited to Israel (Luke 4:25–27); compare John the Baptist's words on God's ability to raise up new children to Abraham (Luke 3:8) and the parable of the vineyard (Matt. 21:33–46 and pars.).

15. See, for example, Jesus' extolling of the centurion's faith (Matt. 5:13 and pars.), as well as the case of the man born blind (John 9).

16. Paul carries on this practice in his scathing rebukes of the Corinthians and their "super-apostles" (1 Cor. 4:8–13; 2 Cor. 12:8–10), and James is, if anything, even more explicit on God's preference for the poor (James 2:17).

17. See, in this context, the evaluations of suffering that surface in the story of the man born blind, in John 9:2, 34.

18. Note, in this context, the reactions to Jesus recorded by the evangelists in Matt. 12:24 and par.; Mark 3:21; John 7:20; 8:48; Mark 2:6–12 and pars.; as well as the various accounts of Jesus' trial before Pilate and the Sanhedrin.

19. Cited by Dwight N. Hopkins, "Slave Theology in the 'Invisible Institution,'" in *Cut Loose Your Stammering Tongue: Black Theology in the Slave Narratives* (Maryknoll, N.Y.: Orbis, 1991), 34. Hopkins continues with the following reflections: "Why were the woods so full of runaways, slaves who defined their humanity as more than white folks' private property and no less than as free children of God? Because the One who offered freedom to oppressed humanity tarried there on the boundaries of society in opposition to the whitewashed columns of the slave masters' residences. Therefore African American bondservants sought to exist with . . . Jesus, who had conquered Satan's evil hold on all humanity, in 'de wilderness.'"

20. "The Jesus movement in Palestine does not totally reject the validity of the Temple and Torah as symbols of Israel's election, but offers an alternative interpretation of them by focusing on the people itself as the locus of God's power and presence" (Fiorenza, *In Memory of Her,* 120).

21. Leonardo Boff, *Church: Charism and Power: Liberation Theology and the Institutional Church* (New York: Crossroad, 1985), 138–43. While Boff's terminology is helpful, it is based on a substantially different analysis than the one given here. Boff sees the distinction between teaching and learning as "two adjectives that describe two practices of the whole community" (p. 139), with the implication that the semipermanent sociological manifestation of these features in clergy and laity is theologically illegitimate. According to the present argument, however, the fact that the whole church is called to listen and to teach derives from the recognition that sociological distinction between center and periphery has a theological basis in the career of Jesus. Regarding Boff's concern that the distinction between center and periphery will lead to a "pathological" imbalance of power in the community, see chapter 5.

22. Following this line of argument, Luther insists that the preservation of church order is a necessary consequence of the priesthood of all believers: "Because we are all priests of equal standing, no one must push himself forward and take it upon himself, without our consent and election, to do that for which we all have equal authority. For no one dare take upon himself what is common to all without the authority and consent of the community" (Luther, "To the Christian Nobility," 129).

23. Dietrich Bonhoeffer makes this point well: "Subjectively the individual's constant link with the congregation arises from his recognition of God's will to speak in the empirical church, from . . . awareness of belonging to the community whose office is to preach the Word, and which is itself the object of the preaching. There is an organic link between the congregation and the individual, brought about by the gratitude of the latter to the mother who gave him life, and by his love for her, along with the confidence that she will constantly bestow gifts on him. Lastly, there is his firm hope that he will again and again, in concrete form, receive the assurance that he is in the church of God and receive his grace" (*Communion of Saints,* 159).

Compare the following: "The will for the church is necessary, but genuine only in connection with, or when arising from, faith in the church which is really present, already established by God" (ibid.).

24. It is because of this interdependence of center and margin that I prefer to speak of God's action in the community as working "from the outside in" rather than "from the bottom up." Opposition of top and bottom seems to me to lead to a hierarchicalization in which one or the other extreme comes to be viewed as superfluous at best (as the bottom seems in the top-down approach which has dominated the understanding of doctrine in the established churches) and illegitimate at worst (as the top sometimes appears in some liberationist views). Thus, while I share liberation theologians' conviction that Jesus' identification with the marginalized is integral to a scripturally based understanding of doctrine, I wish to emphasize that the insights generated at the margins only fulfill their God-given intention of witness to the community as a whole if they are directed to a center that holds. Needless to say, "center" in this context does not refer to a position on the political spectrum, but to a sociological location in the community: the point is not that the Christian God is a God of compromise (far from it!), but a God of unity (Eph. 4:4–6; cf. 1 Cor. 12:4–7).

25. It is, of course, always possible that one party may compel another by force, but the very fact that force is necessary suggests that the one party does not view itself as responsible to the other.

26. This point is in no way compromised by the recognition that the most pointed critiques of established practice may come from the community's margins. Even as the "lost sheep" to whom Jesus is sent are "lost" only from the perspective of their membership in the house of Israel, so the marginalized in general are marginal only in terms of their participation in the larger community. As soon as the marginalized leave the community altogether, they are no longer peripheral members, but simply nonmembers. And while nonmembers may object to the church's practice on any number of counts, the fact that they do not recognize themselves as members of the community suggests that they will have no particular interest in trying to justify their position on the community's terms.

27. Pierre Bourdieu offers a particularly trenchant analysis of the ways in which communal practice, even when ostensibly governed by "objective" rules, in fact functions to safeguard existing relationships of super- and subordination. Bourdieu argues that the very act of appealing to established rules is the product of particular interests which combine to render their own operation as such invisible to participants: "The explanation agents may provide of their own practice, thanks to a quasi-theoretical reflection on their practice, conceals, even from their own eyes, the true nature of their practical mastery, i.e., that it is *learned igno-rance* . . . a mode of practical knowledge not comprising knowledge of its own principles" (Pierre Bourdieu, *Outline of a Theory of Practice,* trans. Richard Nice [Cambridge: Cambridge University Press, 1977], 19).

6. THE GROUND OF AUTHORITY IN THE DIVINE LIFE

1. Note the concerns expressed by Jesus' contemporaries in, for example, Mark 2:6–7 and John 10:33.

2. Albert Raboteau has countered this characterization of the logic of liberation theology in his description of the faith of black Christians in America: "African-American Christians believed they were a chosen people, not because they were black, nor because they suffered, but because their history fit the pattern of salvation revealed to them in the Bible" (Albert J. Raboteau, *A Fire in My Bones: Reflections on African-American Religious History* [Boston: Beacon, 1995], 192).

3. "If the Trinity is the doctrine of a God whose very life is a life of sharing,

its clear consequence is that those who claim belief in such a God must live a similar life" (Justo L. Gonzalez, *Mañana: Christian Theology from a Hispanic Perspective* [Nashville, Tenn.: Abingdon, 1990], 114). In this context, Gonzalez notes that the doctrine of the Trinity is an important feature of the defense of socialism made by Catholic bishop Christopher Mwoleka of Tanzania.

4. Gonzalez, *Mañana,* 111.

5. Patricia Wilson-Kastner, *Faith, Feminism and the Christ* (Philadelphia: Fortress, 1983), 131–33.

6. Leondardo Boff, *Trinity and Society* (Maryknoll, N.Y.: Orbis, 1988); see especially 129–54.

7. See especially LaCugna's review of the problems associated with trinitarian language, as well as some proposed solutions in "God in Communion with Us," in *Freeing Theology: The Essentials of Theology in Feminist Perspective,* ed. Catherine Mowry LaCugna (San Francisco: HarperCollins, 1993), 84–85, 100–105.

8. LaCugna points out: "One of the lessons to be learned from the history of trinitarian theology is that metaphysical positions must be rooted in and derived from what we know of God as revealed in the economy of salvation. Otherwise, metaphysical claims about God will appear to be nothing more than projections of human values onto the divine being. These projections can take the form of a hierarchically ordered or an egalitarian social arrangement. In both cases, what is usually missing is a firm basis in salvation history—in the person of Jesus Christ—for a particular vision of human society" ("God in Communion with Us," 91).

Compare Catherine Mowry LaCugna, *God for Us: The Trinity and Christian Life* (San Francisco: HarperCollins, 1993), 276–78.

9. Therefore, if Christians, too, presume to call God "Father," it is only because Jesus has identified his destiny with theirs (Matt. 10:40; Luke 10:16; John 14:20; Heb. 2:11; cf. Rom. 8:15–17; Eph. 1:5).

10. See the controversies described in John's Gospel (8:13–19; cf. 5:31–38) with respect to the question of Jesus' witnessing to himself.

11. To the above examples could also be added the words of God's messengers in the infancy narratives, especially Matt. 1:20–21 and Luke 1:30–33, 35.

12. The difficulty that Christians have had in accepting this fact is apparent in the Gospel of Matthew, where the evangelist is careful to preface the cry of dereliction with the following words of Jesus: "Do you imagine that I cannot appeal to my Father, and he will at once send me more than twelve legions of angels? But how then would the Scriptures be fulfilled, that these things must be?" (26:53–54).

13. Compare Bonhoeffer's observation that in Jesus Christ, "God lets himself be pushed out of the world on to the cross. He is weak and powerless in the world, and that is precisely the way, the only way in which he is with us and helps us. Matt. 8:17 makes it quite clear that Christ helps us, not by virtue of his omnipotence, but by virtue of his weakness and suffering" (Dietrich Bonhoeffer, *Letters and Papers from Prison,* ed. Eberhard Bethge [London: SCM, 1967], 196).

14. Jürgen Moltmann, *The Trinity and the Kingdom: The Doctrine of God* (San Francisco: Harper & Row, 1981), 81; compare Jürgen Moltmann, *The Crucified God: The Cross of Christ as the Foundation and Criticism of Christian Theology,* trans. R. A. Wilson and John Bowden (Minneapolis: Fortress Press, 1993), 243. Compare Karl Barth's remarks on the suffering of the Father in *CD* IV.2, 357.

15. Jon Sobrino puts it this way: "God's silence on the cross, which causes natural reason and modern reason so much scandal, is not scandalous for the crucified

[in history]. Their crucial concern is whether God was with Jesus on the cross. If the answer is yes, then God's nearness to human beings, initiated in the incarnation, proclaimed and rendered present by Jesus during his earthly life, is consummated. The cross says, in human language, that nothing in history has set limits to God's nearness to human beings. Without that nearness, God's power in the resurrection would remain pure otherness and therefore ambiguous, and, for the crucified, historically threatening. But with that nearness, the crucified can really believe that God's power is good news, for it is love" (Sobrino, *Jesus in Latin America*, 153).

16. The resurrection is thus of a different order than the resuscitation of Lazarus (John 11) or the son of the widow of Nain (Luke 7).

17. "The distinctive humanity of Jesus was constituted by his relation to the Father mediated by the Spirit. In his life, death, resurrection, and ascension is to be discerned the eschatological action of God the Spirit, who thus perfected God's particular humanity in space and time" (Colin E. Gunton, *The One, the Three, and the Many: God, Creation and the Culture of Modernity, The Bampton Lectures 1992* [Cambridge: Cambridge University Press, 1993], 205).

18. "To exist as a person is to be referred to others; the negation and dissolution of personhood is total self-reference" (LaCugna, *God for Us*, 289). Compare Wolfhart Pannenberg, *Systematic Theology* (Grand Rapids: William B. Eerdmans, 1991), 1:426–27, 430. Elizabeth Johnson has pointed out that this understanding is also implicit in Aquinas's definition of the persons *as* "subsistent relations": "This means that the persons are persons precisely as mutual relations and not as anything else apart from their mutual bonding. Relationality is the principle that at once constitutes each trinitarian person as unique and distinguishes one from another. . . . Their uniqueness arises only from their *esse ad*, from their being toward the others in relation" (Elizabeth A. Johnson, *She Who Is: The Mystery of God in Feminist Theological Discourse* [New York: Crossroad, 1992], 216).

19. Using the language of the Cappadocians, LaCugna summarizes this logic of the interdependence of the three persons as follows: "To exist as God is to be the Father who begets the Son and breathes forth the Spirit. Therefore, from one perspective, divine ousia is identical with the Father [but only] as the source of the hypostatic existence of Son and Spirit. From another perspective, divine *ousia* is identical with each person. . . . The heart of the doctrine of the Trinity lies here. The definition of divine persons as relations of origin means that to be a person is to be defined by where a person comes from; *what a person is in itself or by itself cannot be determined*. The Father comes from no one, the Son is begotten of the Father, the Spirit proceeds from the Father. The idea of relation of origin makes it impossible to think of a divine person 'unto itself,' disconnected either from other persons or from the divine essence" (*God for Us*, 69).

20. Indeed, so closely is the Spirit connected with the risen that Paul feels able to move freely between talk of "the Spirit of [God]" and of God who "is the Spirit" (2 Cor. 3:17; cf. Gal. 4:6).

21. See Barth, *CD*, IV.1, 735–39.

22. In this context, Colin Gunton characterizes the work of the Spirit as crossing—while respecting—boundaries: "Spirit relates to one another beings and realms that are opposed or separate. That which is or has spirit is able to be open to that which is other than itself, to move into relation with the other. It is particularly but not only used of God and the world. By his Spirit God comes into relationship with the world. . . . The result of this movement is that by his Spirit God enables creation to be open to him" (*The One, the Three, and the Many*, 181–82).

23. In the same way, one might argue that while a marriage is not any less a marriage where there are no children, a marriage is undoubtedly enriched by the presence of children.

24. The falsehood of the serpent's words are nowhere more apparent than when it is recognized that the desire to be independent of relationship with God is profoundly undivine in light of God's own internal relationality.

25. In this context, Gunton argues that the Spirit "far from abolishing, rather strengthens and maintains particularity. It is not a Spirit of merging or assimilation—of homogenization—but of relation in otherness, relation which does not subvert but establishes the other in true reality" (*The One, the Three, and the Many*, 182).

26. See especially Luke 24:25–27; Matt. 13:10–15; 21:4 and pars.; John 2:17, 22.

27. Barth, *CD*, I.2, 625.

28. Ibid., I.2, 698.

7. AUTHORITY AND THE POWER OF NAMING

1. As both Elisabeth Schüssler Fiorenza and Elizabeth Johnson have shown, this tendency toward masculinization emerged very early in church practice and involved the active subversion of preexisting female imagery for the divine. Indeed, Johnson argues that the identification of Jesus with the female figure of divine Wisdom (Sophia), of which only traces remain in the canonical New Testament (see, e.g., Matt. 11:19 and par.; Luke 11:49; 1 Cor. 1:24), may have been integral to the process by which Christians came to conceive Jesus as existing in an ontologically unique relationship with God. See Elizabeth A. Johnson, "Redeeming the Name of Christ," in *Freeing Theology*, ed. LaCugna, 121; cf. Elisabeth Schüssler Fiorenza, *Jesus: Miriam's Child, Sophia's Prophet: Critical Issues in Feminist Christology* (New York: Continuum, 1994), 139–54.

2. Fiorenza has proposed the term "kyriarchy" as better suited than "patriarchy" to describe the multiple and interrelated patterns of domination and submission through which elite males keep both women and most men subordinate to them (Elisabeth Schüssler Fiorenza, *But She Said: Feminist Practices of Biblical Interpretation* [Boston: Beacon, 1992], 115–17; cf. Fiorenza, *Jesus: Miriam's Child*, 14).

3. Sandra Schneiders, *Women and the Word* (New York: Paulist, 1986), 48; cited in LaCugna, "God in Communion," 104.

4. Johnson, "Redeeming the Name of Christ," 120.

5. Rosemary Radford Ruether, *Sexism and God-Talk* (Boston: Beacon, 1983), 137; compare the following: "On this reading Jesus' maleness is prophecy announcing from within the end of patriarchy, at least as divinely ordained" (Johnson, "Redeeming the Name of Christ," 127).

6. While variations on this line of reasoning recur throughout the history of Christian thought, perhaps its most notorious manifestation in the modern period is found in the anthropology Karl Barth outlines in the third volume of his *Church Dogmatics*: "The sum of all truth and actuality, which is thus also the beginning and end of all things, the secret of creation and its consummation, is the very different duality merely reflected in the [sexual] nature of man—that of God and man in their co-existence in the concrete form of the covenant established between Himself and His people Israel. This duality . . . is the original of which the essence of the human as man and woman can only be the reflection and copy. Man is primarily and properly Yahweh, and woman primarily and properly Israel" (Barth, *CD*, III.2, 297).

7. See Fiorenza's review of feminist discussion of the theology of the cross in *Jesus: Miriam's Child,* 98–107.

8. "The orthodox doctrine of the Trinity . . . makes it plain that subordination is unnatural, contrary to the nature and destiny of all personhood, divine and human" (LaCugna, "God in Communion," 94); compare LaCugna, *God for Us,* 299–300. Note that it is to preserve the full equality of the divine persons that Jesus' statement "the Father is greater than I" (John 14:28) is classically attributed to his human nature.

9. Though Paul goes on in the next verse to speak of the subjection of the Son to the Father, he makes it clear that this is a future event that signals the end of the Son's mission. In other words, sending is not a matter of subjection, but the mode of the Son's empowerment. The subjection of the Son to the Father, by contrast, pertains rather to the Son's eschatological return as victorious Sovereign and the process whereby the Son freely returns the divine rule to the one who consigned it to the Son.

10. Fiorenza, *In Memory of Her,* 150. Compare the observation, in reference to Mark 3:35, that "those who live the gracious goodness of God are Jesus' true family, which includes brothers, sisters, and mothers, but significantly enough, no fathers" (ibid., 147).

11. Thus, we may agree with the author of 1 John's definition of the Antichrist as "the one who denies the Father and the Son" (1 John 2:22) without thereby tying the validity of our confession to the exclusive use of a particular set of words. On the contrary, if the argument presented here is correct, the church will fail to affirm the relationship signified in the Bible by the terms "Father" and "Son" if it insists that only these words succeed in identifying the biblical God.

12. For a helpful summary of the narrative requirements of a distinctively Christian naming of God, see Christopher Morse, *Not Every Spirit: A Dogmatics of Christian Disbelief* (Valley Forge, Pa.: Trinity Press International, 1994), 134, 138.

13. Compare Jesus' warning that those who seek to save their lives will lose them (Matt. 16:25 and pars.).

14. Fiorenza notes that the "empty tomb" Easter traditions in particular stress the this-worldly implications of Jesus' resurrection: "the proclamation of the empty tomb locates the Resurrected One on earth, in Galilee. Resurrection means that Jesus, the Living One, goes ahead of us" (*Jesus: Miriam's Child,* 123).

15. In the same way, Paul's exclamation "O the depth of the riches and the wisdom and the knowledge of God! How unsearchable are [God's] judgments and how inscrutable [God's] ways!" (Rom. 11:33) is not prompted by confusion or uncertainly, but by the sure conviction that despite the appearances of the moment, it is God's firm intent to show mercy to all—especially to those who at present seem especially recalcitrant.

16. One might consider this point a modern reformulation of the Scholastic idea that God is pure act. From this perspective, the suggestion that God might have acted differently than God did, far from enhancing the divine freedom, diminishes it by implying that God was at some time impeded in the realization of God's self by being forced to consider between different courses of action. By contrast, the biblical narratives portray a God who hesitates before various possibilities: "God is not a . . . mortal, that [God] should change [God's] mind" (Num. 23:19). Compare Karl Rahner, *Foundations of Christian Faith: An Introduction to the Idea of Christianity* (New York: Crossroad, 1992), 38: "When freedom is really

understood, it is not the power to be able to do this or that, but the power to decide about oneself and actualize oneself."

17. "There are not two sets of communion—one among the divine persons, the other among human persons, with the latter supposed to replicate the former. The one perichoresis, the one mystery of communion, includes God and humanity as beloved partners in the dance" (LaCugna, *God for Us*, 274).

18. So Paul states that he has been entrusted with the task of preaching the gospel in order that "the manifold wisdom of God might be made known at the present time *through the church* to the powers and authorities in the heavenly places" (Eph. 3:10).

19. Thus, what Justo Gonzalez says about Jesus in particular may be applied, through Jesus, to the relationship between divine and human exercise of authority in general: "Divine and human are not two opposite poles . . . so that as one approaches one pole one moves away from the other. Being more human does not make Jesus less divine. And being more divine does not make him less human. Actually, it is precisely in his being for others that Jesus manifests his full divinity, and it is also in his being for others that he manifests his full humanity" (Gonzalez, *Mañana,* 152).

20. "The authorization of theological discourse about Jesus, who was executed as the Christ, who was vindicated by God as the Living One, and who is always ahead of us, does not derive its authority from 'revelatory' . . . experiences. Rather it must be articulated and proven 'right' again and again within the continuing struggles for survival, justice, and well-being" (Fiorenza, *Jesus: Miriam's Child,* 127–28).

21. As Cone puts it: "[The] prioritizing [of black liberation] does not mean that Black Theology makes the experience of Christ secondary to the experience of black oppression. Rather it means that black people have come to know Christ precisely through oppression, because he has made himself synonymous with black oppression. Therefore, to deny the reality of black oppression and to affirm some other 'reality' is to deny Christ" (*Black Theology and Black Power,* 120). Compare the following: "Because Black Theology has as its starting point the Black condition, this does not mean that it denies the absolute revelation of God in Christ. Rather, it means that Black theology firmly believes that God's revelation in Christ can be made supreme only by affirming Christ as he is alive in black people today" (ibid., 118).

INDEX